Special Edition

Living Bibles International

How to Grow

First Steps for New Christians

Kenneth N. Taylor

OLIVER NELSON

A Division of Thomas Nelson Publishers

Nashville • Atlanta • Camden • New York

Published in Nashville, Tennessee, by Oliver-Nelson Books, a division
of Thomas Nelson, Inc., Publishers, and distributed in Canada by
Lawson Falle, Ltd., Cambridge, Ontario.
Scripture quotations noted NKJV are from the NEW KING JAMES
VERSION. Copyright © 1979, 1980, 1982, Thomas Nelson, Inc.,
Publishers.
Scripture quotations noted TLB are from *The Living Bible* (Wheaton, Il-
linois: Tyndale House Publishers, 1971) and are used by permission.
Printed in the United States of America.

Library of Congress Cataloging in Publication Data
Taylor, Kenneth Nathaniel.
  How to grow.

  Includes bibliographical references.
  1. Christian life—1960-   I. Title.
BV4501.2.T29   1985   248.4   85-11512
ISBN 0-8407-9038-4

Contents

PART FOUR
Fulfilling God's Plan

PART FIVE
Facing Some Issues

PART ONE

Knowing
God's Love

Chapter One

For it is the God who commanded light to shine out of darkness who has shone in our hearts to give the light of the knowledge of the glory of God in the face of Jesus Christ.

2 Corinthians 4:6 NKJV

The Greatest Decision

Congratulations! You have made the greatest decision you can ever make: You have decided for God! You have asked Jesus to save you. You have accepted the greatest gift that ever was or ever can be—the gift of eternal life. You have been born again.

Let me remind you of how this all came about, for it is a wonderful story and you should never lose the wonder of it. You were headed downhill to eternal death and doom, trapped, as Satan's prisoner, subject to his dark will and destiny, and suddenly the chains were snapped, the blindfold lifted from your eyes, and the invisible hands knocked off you. Now a new, free world waits before you.

Well, what happened to set you free?

God Loves You

It all began because God loves you. He always has loved you. He always has wanted you as His child, wanted to be a loving Father to you. But there was a problem.

You were (and are) a sinner. I don't know anything

about your personal sins, but you do and God does. Nothing is hidden from Him. He knows your inner evil thoughts as well as any secret sinful actions, and God can't tolerate sin of any kind in heaven. How can you spend forever with Him, the glorious, holy God, if your life is filled with wickedness? He simply won't allow it.

So are we all in a hopeless plight? Yes, *except for the way God arranged to forgive our sins*. If our sins are forgiven, then He can accept us. Now *your* sins are forgiven, and God has wiped them out. Your slate is clean. You have a spotless record with Him. "For the wages of sin is death, but the gift of God is eternal life in Christ Jesus our Lord."[1]

What Happened?

How did this glorious fact occur? How can sins be forgiven? What happened is this: No human being is good enough to get into heaven, let alone get you and me in too. The Bible says, "No one is good—no one in all the world is innocent."[2] The only person good enough is God's child, Jesus Christ. He had no sin of any kind at any time. The Scriptures declare that He "was in all points tempted as we are, yet without sin."[3]

Only Jesus is worthy of heaven. Only He can get us into heaven too. But first our sins must be washed away. Even Jesus Christ can't get us in until we are cleaned up in God's sight. For reasons not entirely clear, God can't just forgive us without a sacrificial death. Someone had to die for us, and the only death God could accept on our behalf

1. Romans 6:23 NKJV
2. Romans 3:10 TLB
3. Hebrews 4:15 NKJV

was the death of His Son Jesus. "Christ also suffered. He died once for the sins of all us guilty sinners, although he himself was innocent of any sin at any time, that he might bring us safely home to God."[4]

The Miracle of Salvation

But would God be willing to see His very own Son die—the child He loves so very dearly? Would His Son be willing to undergo the tortures of hell in our place? The answer is, simply, yes to both questions.

Was God willing? Yes! "For God so loved the world that He gave His only begotten Son, that whoever believes in Him should not perish but have everlasting life."[5]

Was Jesus willing? Yes! "...overwhelming victory is ours through Christ who loved us enough to die for us."[6]

> Now God says he will accept us and acquit us—declare us "not guilty"—if we trust Jesus Christ to take away our sins. And we all can be saved in this same way, by coming to Christ, no matter who we are or what we have been like. Yes, all have sinned; all fall short of God's glorious ideal; yet now God declares us "not guilty" of offending him if we trust in Jesus Christ, who in his kindness freely takes away our sins. For God sent Christ Jesus to take the punishment for our sins and to end all God's anger against us.[7]

And so God's Son came to earth to die for us. He came in the form of a human body, born to a virgin named Mary, and grew up as a normal boy and young man (except that He had no sin). When He was thirty years old He began His three-year public ministry of preaching and

4. 1 Peter 3:18 TLB
5. John 3:16 NKJV
6. Romans 8:37 TLB
7. Romans 3:22–25 TLB

healing, and then He was killed by the religious leaders of His day—and in His death He died for our sins, yours and mine. (Not His own, for remember, He didn't have any.)

That one act opened up the gates of heaven for you because you have accepted His friendship and have asked Him to include you among those for whom He died. How glad Jesus is, and so is God in heaven. All the angels broke into songs of joy and praise when it was announced that you had accepted God's wonderful offer of eternal salvation.

A New Birthday

What a day that was for heaven and for you! It became your new birthday—the day when you were born again. That day marked the beginning of your opportunities to please God in everything you do here on earth, for all the years (many or few) that God will give to you before welcoming you into your new eternal home.

Now that you belong to God, what joys there are for you, both in this life and in the life awaiting you in heaven. What a contrast to the old, often frustrating life you used to live!

Chapter Two

And we know that all things work together for good to those who love God, to those who are the called according to His purpose.

Romans 8:28 NKJV

The Fruit of the Spirit

Good-Bye to the Old Life

I had an experience recently that clearly called to my attention the vast difference between the old nature and the new nature. Tim, a friend of mine, was driving from Wisconsin to my home near Chicago. Along the way, he picked up a hitchhiker whose name was John. John's car had broken down the previous evening, and in temperatures hovering near zero, John and his dog had walked the ten miles back to their trailer home. His wife had recently departed after a stormy five years of marriage, but they were still friends, he said, and he had come to Chicago to borrow her car, since she lived on a bus route and it was hard for her to find parking in her neighborhood. The two men arrived at my home near suppertime, and I invited John to stay and eat with us before taking the suburban train for the brief remainder of his trip. Of course, he was happy to accept my invitation.

After supper John and I talked awhile before I took him to the train station. John told me he was an alcoholic who could go for several weeks without a drink and then he would fall apart and be drunk for several days on end. He was trying Alcoholics Anonymous, but he wasn't sure yet whether that was helping him. As we sat before the fireplace I asked him to read aloud from the Bible I opened for him, and he did. This is what he read:

> When you follow your own wrong inclinations your lives will produce these evil results: impure thoughts, eagerness for lustful pleasure, idolatry, spiritism (that is, encouraging the activity of demons), hatred and fighting, jealousy and anger, constant effort to get the best for yourself, complaints and criticisms, the feeling that everyone else is wrong except those in your own little group—and there will be wrong doctrine, envy, murder, drunkenness, wild parties, and all that sort of thing. Let me tell you again as I have before, that anyone living that sort of life will not inherit the kingdom of God.[1]

"Does any of this description fit you, John?" I asked.

"Yes," he said, "most of it. How I wish I could get rid of all of it."

"Well, read on," I told him.

So he read: "But when the Holy Spirit controls our lives he will produce this kind of fruit in us: love, joy, peace, patience, kindness, goodness, faithfulness, gentleness and self-control."[2]

"How does that sound to you?" I asked him.

"Absolutely wonderful," he replied. "I'd give anything to be like that."

Then I had the privilege of telling John the incredible fact that when you turn your life over to God and ask

1. Galatians 5:19–21 TLB
2. Galatians 5:22 TLB

Jesus Christ to come into your heart and life, He brings the Holy Spirit with Him, and together with God the Father and Jesus our Lord they clean out the rubbish and bring in the light and joy from heaven. What a deal! To trade the old unhappy life set on a disaster course for a joyful life filled with good things, a new life leading straight to heaven.

My Story

Let me tell you about how it happened in my own life. I was brought up in a strong Christian home where God was honored deeply. Our family read the Bible together every day and each one of us prayed. I became a Christian at a time earlier than I can remember. I didn't go through the so-called rebellious teens. I respected my parents and was glad to try to please them. My college days were busy and happy. Perhaps the only unusual thing about them was the fact that I went to a Christian school, which had revival weeks twice a year. I was often challenged to turn my life over to God, and I tried to do this.

Now, as I look back at my efforts, I realize I was always clutching a few keys to rooms in my life: I was unwilling to let go of them and give them to Christ. So I experienced some progress, but in a stumbling sort of way. I didn't want to let go of things such as popularity, or a medical or legal career in the future that would lead to wealth and respect. One thing I especially didn't want was to be a pastor or a missionary. I kept those keys—the right to make these choices—in my pocket. As a result I went through a lot of unhappiness and depression and jealousy. God was saying, "Let go. I must have *those* keys too." But I was saying, "No!"

It was during the summer of my junior year in college

that I finally let them go. One Sunday afternoon I was reading a biography of Bill Borden, a Yale University student many years ago. He was a very unusual man in several ways. He was an excellent student and was on the varsity wrestling team. He was strong spiritually too; he used to go down to a city rescue mission (similar to those the Salvation Army operates) and preach to the alcoholics and other homeless men there, telling them of God's love for them and urging them to let God rescue them and give them useful lives again.

To me one of the most interesting facts about Bill Borden was that his father had been a millionaire and had left his fortune to Bill. But I was unsettled when I learned that Bill gave away his inheritance to missionary societies and other Christian projects so that more people would hear and accept the good news. He did not keep it all for himself.

Then came an even heavier blow: I read that Bill decided to become a missionary. Here was a man I had grown to like and respect as I read the book about him, and he did two important things in exactly the opposite direction of my plans. My plans, remember, were never to be a missionary and to become wealthy! In contrast, Bill gave away his money and became a missionary. My conscience hit me hard. I knew that I too should be willing to do whatever God wanted me to, and not hold out on these points or any others. But I wouldn't let go.

Didn't I realize what a fool I was—to try to run my own life when God was willing to run it for me? Yes, but God might not let me have the things I wanted in life. And, of course, I was right: He probably wouldn't. What I wanted was for myself, not for God and for others.

The Choice

I faced the problem many others faced then and now. You may be facing it too. Who is going to be in charge of your life? You? Or God?

If you decide to run your life without God's direction, you will have half a chance (or less) of achieving your goals. Hard work with a positive attitude can sometimes work wonders. Notice I said *sometimes*. But if you succeed, and get to the top of the ladder, will you find you are at the top of the wrong wall? Probably so.

How do you find the right wall to climb? First, *know* God's will for your life. Then *do* it. To spend your life rushing after your own goals is eternal foolishness. It is eternal because a judgment day is coming when eternal rewards will be passed out by Christ the King, and it will be true that those Christians who are the first and most important on earth may be the least appreciated in heaven. They are children of God, but they will be coming with wasted lives, offering them to Him in shame.

Well, I've gotten ahead of my story. As I read on in the book about Bill Borden, puzzled and dismayed by his decision to let God run his life, I learned that only a few weeks after arriving in Cairo, Egypt, to begin his work as a missionary to the Arab world, he woke up one morning feeling sick and had to stay in bed because of a high fever. The fever didn't go away, but became worse. It looked as though Bill might die.

I had heard and read enough missionary stories to know how God sometimes heals people, so I was completely unprepared to find out that God didn't heal Bill. Instead, Bill died. I was utterly shocked. Bill had given everything to God—wealth, opportunity, everything—only to have God snuff out his life!

God was unfair. God was ungrateful. *I would never serve a God like that,* I thought. So I decided, as I sat there reading, to go my own way and run my own life instead of entrusting it to God. I turned my back on Him and His safe path, and I spiritually stepped over the cliff to plunge to the rocks below.

God's Mercy

Then a strange thing happened. God had mercy on me. Even as I was defying Him and deciding to go my own way and do my own thing, my mind changed and I saw the fatal foolishness of that decision. A moment later I was down on my knees beside the chair where I had been reading. And I found myself praying and telling God that He could have my life, and I would do whatever He wanted me to do. It was as though He reached out for me as I was going over the edge and pulled me back and gave me a second chance.

From then on, although with some bumps, relapses, and detours along the way, I have stuck to my goal: to belong to Him alone and to be what He wants me to be, to do what He tells me to do. What happiness and joy I have had as a result!

What if I had insisted on going my own way? I might (or might not) have been reasonably happy and successful in my earthly life, but my eternal rewards would be lost. And the joy of living for God in this life would never be mine.

Jesus said,

> All who listen to my instructions and follow them are wise, like a man who builds his house on solid rock. Though the

rain comes in torrents, and the floods rise and the storm winds beat against his house, it won't collapse, for it is built on rock.

But those who hear my instructions and ignore them are foolish, like a man who builds his house on sand. For when the rains and floods come, and storm winds beat against his house, it will fall with a mighty crash.[3]

3. Matthew 7:24–27 TLB

Chapter Three

Be of good courage, and He shall strengthen your heart, all you who hope in the Lord.

Psalm 31:24 NKJV

My Heart, Christ's Home

Many years ago I heard a story that has ever left its grip on me, a story about turning over one's life to Christ, letting Him have complete control. Here is the story[1] as retold by a friend of mine:

One evening I invited Jesus Christ into my heart. What an entrance He made! It was not a spectacular emotional thing, but very real. It was at the very center of my life. He came into the darkness of my heart and turned on the light. He built a fire on the hearth and banished the chill. He started music where there had been stillness, and He filled the emptiness with His own loving, wonderful fellowship. I have never regretted opening the door to Christ and I never will—not into eternity!

In the joy of this newfound relationship I said to Jesus Christ, "Lord, I want this heart of mine to be Yours. I want You to settle down here and be perfectly at home.

---

1. Taken from *My Heart—Christ's Home* by Robert Munger. © 1954 by Inter-Varsity Christian Fellowship of the USA and used by permission of InterVarsity Press, Downers Grove, IL 60515.

Everything I have belongs to You. Let me show You around."

The Library

The first room was the study—the library. In my home this room of the mind is a very small room with very thick walls, but it is a very important room. In a sense, it is the control room of the house. He entered with me and looked around at the books in the bookcases, the magazines on the table, the pictures on the wall. As I followed His gaze I became uncomfortable.

Strangely, I had not felt self-conscious about this before, but now that He was there looking at these things I was embarrassed. Some books were there that His eyes were too pure to behold. There was a lot of trash and literature on the table that a Christian had no business reading, and as for the pictures on the wall—the imaginations and thoughts of the mind—some of them were shameful.

I turned to Him and said, "Master, I know that this room needs some radical alterations. Will You help me make it what it ought to be, and bring every thought into captivity to You?"

"Certainly," He said. "First of all, take all the things that you are reading and looking at which are not helpful, pure, good and true, and throw them out. Now put on the empty shelves the books of the Bible. Fill the library with Scripture and 'meditate therein day and night' (Joshua 1:8). As for the pictures on the wall, you will have difficulty controlling these images, but there is an aid." He gave me a full-sized portrait of Himself. "Hang this centrally," He said, "on the wall of the mind."

I did so, and I have discovered through the years that when my attention is centered upon Christ Himself, His purity and power cause impure imaginings to retreat. So He has helped me to bring my thoughts into captivity.

The Dining Room

From the study we went into the dining room, the room of appetites and desires. I spent a good deal of time here and put forth much effort in satisfying my wants. I said to Him, "This is a very big room, and I am quite sure You will be pleased with what we serve."

He seated Himself at the table with me and asked, "What is on the menu for dinner?"

"Well," I said, "my favorite dishes: old bones, corn husks, sour garbage, leeks, onions, and garlic right out of Egypt." These were the things I liked—worldly fare.

When the food was placed before Him, He said nothing, but I observed that He did not eat it. I said to Him, "Master, You don't care for this food? What is the trouble?"

He answered, "I have meat to eat that you know not of.... If you want food that really satisfies, seek the will of the Father, not your own pleasures, not your own desires, not your own satisfaction. Seek to please Me. That food will satisfy you." There at the table He gave me a taste of the joy of doing God's will. What a flavor! *What nourishment and vitality it gives the soul!* There is no food like it in all the world. It alone satisfies.

The Drawing Room

From the dining room we walked into the drawing room. This room was intimate and comfortable. I liked it. It had a fireplace, upholstered chairs, a sofa, and a quiet atmosphere. He said, "This is indeed a delightful room. Let us come

23

here often. It is secluded and quiet, and we can have fellowship together."

Well, as a young Christian I was thrilled. I could not think of anything I would rather do than have a few minutes apart with Christ in intimate fellowship.

He promised, "I will be here early every morning. Meet Me here, and we will start the day together."

Morning after morning, I would come downstairs to the drawing room, or "withdrawing room," as I liked to think of it. He would take a book of the Bible from the case. We would open it and read together. He would tell me of its richness and unfold to me its truths. My heart warmed as He revealed the love and the grace He had toward me. These were wonderful hours.

Little by little, under the pressure of my many responsibilities, the time began to be shortened. Why, I don't know, but I thought I was too busy to spend time with Christ. This was not intentional, you understand. It just happened that way. Finally, not only was the time shortened, but I began to miss a day now and then. Perhaps it was some other pressing need. I would miss it two days in a row and oftentimes more.

I remember one morning when I was rushing downstairs, eager to be on my way, that I passed the drawing room and noticed that the door was ajar. Looking in, I saw a fire in the fireplace and the Master sitting there next to it. Suddenly in dismay I thought to myself, *He is my guest. I invited Him into my heart! He has come and yet I am neglecting Him.*

With downcast glance, I said, "Blessed Master, forgive me. Have You been here all these mornings?"

"Yes," He said, "I told you I would be here every morning to meet with you. Remember, I love you. I have redeemed you at great cost. I desire your fellowship. Even if you cannot keep the quiet time for your own sake, do it for Mine."

The truth that Christ desires my companionship, that He wants me to be with Him and waits for me, has done more to transform my quiet time with God than any other single factor. Don't let Christ wait alone in the drawing room of your heart, but every day find time when, with your Bible and in prayer, you may have fellowship with Him.

The Workshop

Before long, He asked, "Do you have a workshop in your home?" Down in the basement of my heart I had a bench and some equipment, but I was not doing much with it. Once in a while I would go down and fuss around with a few little gadgets, but I wasn't producing anything substantial.

I led Him down there. He looked over the workbench and said, "Well, this is quite well furnished. What are you producing with your life for the kingdom of God?" He looked at one or two little toys that I had thrown together on the bench. He held one up to me and said, "Are these little toys all that you are producing in your Christian life?"

"Well," I said, "Lord, I know it isn't much, and I really want to do more, but after all, I don't seem to have strength or skill to do more."

"Would you like to do better?" He asked.

"Certainly," I replied.

"All right. Let Me have your hands. Now relax in Me and let My Spirit work through you." Stepping around behind me and putting His great, strong hands under mine, holding the tools in His skilled fingers, He began to work through me. The more I relaxed and trusted Him, the more He was able to do with my life.

The Playroom

He asked me if I had a playroom. I was hoping He would not ask about this. There were certain associations and friendships, activities, and amusements that I wanted to keep for myself. One evening when I was leaving to join some college companions, He stopped me with a glance and asked, "Are you going out this evening?"

I replied, "Yes."

"Good," He said. "I would like to go with you."

"Oh," I answered rather awkwardly, "I don't think, Lord Jesus, that You would really want to go with me. Let's go out tomorrow night. Tomorrow night we will go to prayer meeting, but tonight I have another appointment."

"I'm sorry," He said, "I thought that when I came into your home, we were going to do everything together, to be partners. I want you to know that I am willing to go with you."

"Well," I mumbled, slipping out the door, "we will go someplace tomorrow night."

That evening I spent some miserable hours. I felt wretched. What kind of friend was I to Christ when I was deliberately leaving Him out of my associations, doing things and going places that I knew very well He would not enjoy?

When I returned that evening, there was a light in His room, and I went up to talk it over with Him. I said, "Lord, I have learned my lesson. I cannot have a good time without You. We will do everything together." Then we went down into the playroom of the house and He transformed it. He brought new friends into my life, new satisfactions, lasting joys. Laughter and music have been ringing through the house ever since.

The Cupboard

One day I found Him waiting for me at the door. There was an arresting look in His eye, and He said to me as I entered, "There is a peculiar odor in the house. Something is dead around here. It's upstairs. I'm sure it is in the hall cupboard." As soon as He said the words, I knew what He was talking about.

There was a small hall cupboard up there on the landing, just a few feet square. In that cupboard, behind lock and key, I had one or two little personal things that I did not want Christ to see. I knew they were dead and rotting things, but I so wanted them for myself that I was afraid to admit they were there.

I went up with Him, and as we mounted the stairs the odor became stronger and stronger. He pointed to the door. I was angry. That's the only way I can put it. I had given Him access to the library, the dining room, the drawing room, the workshop, and the playroom, and now He was asking me about a little two-by-four cupboard. I said inwardly, "This is too much. I am not going to give Him the key."

Reading my thoughts, He said, "If you think I'm going to stay with this odor, you are mistaken. I will go out on the porch."

I saw Him start down the stairs. My resistance collapsed. When one comes to know and love Christ, the worst thing that can happen is to sense His companionship withdrawing. I had to surrender.

"I'll give You the key," I said sadly, "but You will have

to open up the cupboard and clean it out. I haven't the strength to do it."

"Just give Me the key," He said. "Authorize Me to take care of that cupboard and I will."

With trembling fingers I passed the key to Him. He took it, walked over to the door, opened it, took out all the putrefying stuff that was rotting there, and threw it away. Then He cleaned and painted it. It was done in a moment. Oh, what victory and release to have those dead things out of my life!

The Invitation

A thought came to me. "Lord, is there any chance that You would take over the management of the whole house and operate it for me as You did that cupboard? Would You take the responsibility to keep my life what it ought to be?"

His face lighted up as He replied, "Certainly, that is what I want to do. You cannot be a victorious Christian in your own strength. Let Me do it through you and for you. That is the way. But," He added slowly, "I am just a guest. I have no authority to proceed, since the property is not Mine."

Dropping to my knees, I said, "Lord, You have been a guest and I have been the host. From now on I am going to be the servant. You are going to be the Lord." Running as fast as I could to the strongbox, I took the title deed to the house describing its properties, assets, and liabilities. I eagerly signed the house over to Him alone for time and eternity. "Here," I said. "Here it is, all that I am and have, forever. Now You run the house. I'll just remain with You as a servant and friend."

Things are different since Jesus has settled down and has made His home in my heart.

Chapter Four

"And I will pray the Father, and He will give you another Helper, that He may abide with you forever."

John 14:16 NKJV

Who Is the Holy Spirit and What Does He Do?

When Jesus was talking to His disciples about the fact that He would be killed, come back to life again, and return to His Father in heaven, He told them to wait in Jerusalem for the Holy Spirit to come upon them. He said that when the Holy Spirit came, He would comfort and counsel them and remind them of all that Jesus had taught them.

The Trinity

The Holy Spirit is one of the three persons of the Godhead—the Father, the Son (Jesus), and the Holy Spirit. Yet these are not three Gods. There is one God as three persons. This is the doctrine of the Trinity, and it is not a concept we can easily understand, for we know of no appropriate earthly analogy.

The Apostle Paul tells us that if we do not have the Holy Spirit within us, we do not belong to God and we are not Christians at all. How, then, do we get the Holy Spirit into our lives? He comes in when Christ comes in!

The Spirit's Work

What is His work when He comes into our hearts and lives? We have already mentioned that He comforts us as a close Friend, and He gives us counsel and guidance. If you have been discouraged, sad and lonely, without direction, or depressed and friendless, you no longer need to have such problems. Now the Holy Spirit is in your life. In prayer you can confide in Him, and as you think and pray and read God's Word, you will begin to find peace, comfort, and power. Through these disciplines you are giving the Holy Spirit the opportunity to do all He wants to do for you. "For God has not given us a spirit of fear, but of power and of love and of a sound mind."[1]

You need to know that although the Holy Spirit has been sent to you to help you, you can block His help: "Don't cause the Holy Spirit sorrow by the way you live."[2] "Do not quench the Spirit,"[3] is another heavy warning. How might you grieve and quench the Spirit? By disobeying Him and doing things that make Him sad. When this happens you must confess the sin and reopen your life to God.

The Holy Spirit will automatically take away the rotten things within you if you ask Him to do that, and if you turn them over to Him and let Him deal with them. That is why it is imperative for you to stay in close harmony with the Holy Spirit and to follow His pathway rather than try to drag Him along yours—which is, of course, impossible.

The Holy Spirit's power within us is strong when we are fully committed to God and anxious to obey Him,

1. 2 Timothy 1:7 NKJV
2. Ephesians 4:30 TLB
3. 1 Thessalonians 5:19 NKJV

but we have the ability to turn away from God and thus allow Satan to gain ground. That is why we are warned in the Scriptures not to quench the Spirit and not to grieve the Spirit.

Many a true story can be told of Christians who had the power of God through the Holy Spirit in their lives when they became Christians, and later on they were turned aside from following God by the lures of this world and all its glamour. They wanted their way whether or not it was God's will for them, and their lives became encrusted with hardness against God—for no one can serve two masters, God and money. Then the joy of the Lord departed, and their once promising lives in the eternal purposes of God became debilitated and wasted. Don't let that happen to you.

Staying close to the Savior requires a regular audit of your life by you and the Holy Spirit on a daily basis. Is there a temptation facing you? Face it squarely and cry out to God to help you deal with it. Have you succumbed to a temptation, and is there sin in your life that needs to be confessed? Do it at once so that God can restore you to His fellowship and so that the Holy Spirit's power can return. Then strive to keep this serious situation from happening again, by listening to God's Word as you read it each day and by obeying it. Spend time daily talking with the Lord in prayer. The Bible and prayer are two of the means of grace God has given which you neglect at your peril—to the church's loss and to Christ's sorrow. These disciplines allow the Holy Spirit to be continually active in your life.

But first, let's check on something: *Are you allowing the Holy Spirit to bless you?* For you can destroy His power to help!

PART TWO

Tapping
God's Power

Chapter Five

Winking at sin leads to sorrow; bold reproof leads to peace.
Proverbs 10:10 TLB

The Power of Confession

You are on your way, on a fresh, new pathway, surrounded by God's blessings and His care. Even though this new route still leads through briars and difficulties, and threads its way along the edge of cliffs and chasms and around foul smelling garbage dumps of this world's pleasures and woes, the fresh, springtime wind from heaven keeps you serene and joyful.

A Warning

But now I must warn you. As a new pilgrim setting out on this journey you need to know that you can step off the path, and step out of God's blessing. In other words, you can still sin.

"What?" you may exclaim. "Didn't I leave all that behind when I declared for Christ?" And the answer is yes. But you are a voluntary recruit. You are not chained to God's chariot. You are still free to follow your own inclinations. You can disobey your King.

But who would ever want to disobey Him? We may not really want to disobey, but Satan is there encouraging us to go against God. Who is this person who has such power over the world and over us? He is God's great enemy who goes about as a roaring lion, seeking whom he may devour. Some time in the past of eternity he was the highest of the angels, next in power to the triune God, until he revolted against God. With many of the angels on his side, he despised God and fought against Him, and he was dethroned and cast out of heaven.

Now he and his cohorts, the other fallen angels, are using every device possible to turn away mankind, whom God made for Himself, from following God. He is especially angry with those who turn their lives over to God. You are one of those Satan wants, and he is extremely anxious to help you disobey. Even though you have turned to Christ, he still has a toehold in your heart and over the old nature that once dominated you but now has crept into a corner.

Your old nature is still there, and if you give it a chance by encouraging it, it leaps out, sneering at you and your Lord. It takes over, and you sin in thought, word, or deed. Can this really happen to a child of God? Yes, for the Scriptures declare to Christians, ''If we say that we have no sin, we deceive ourselves.''[1] This is a fact of the Christian life, and God tells us clearly, explicitly, what to do about it. How to get the old nature back into its cage again is part of your manual of instructions—the Bible.

The Answer

The first step is to cry out to God for His forgiveness

---

1. 1 John 1:8 NKJV

and help. He says, "Call upon Me in the day of trouble."[2]

He is always ready to help you cage His enemy. As you call upon God, you are to recognize and admit that you have sinned, and turn from the sin and return to the pathway of God.

"If we confess our sins, He is faithful and just to forgive us our sins and to cleanse us from all unrighteousness."[3] How wonderful is this provision! God knows our weaknesses, and Christ's death for our sins included the sins we commit in the new life, as well as those before we came to Him for our salvation.

Look at this verse again: "He [God] is faithful and just to forgive us our sins and to cleanse us from all unrighteousness [all that is not right]." He is faithful, that is, He doesn't break His promise. And His promise to His Son is that all who receive His Son as Savior become God's children, adopted into His own family. When a child does wrong, he isn't kicked out of the family, though he may be disciplined. This isn't a perfect illustration, because you may know of kids who have been kicked out. But God doesn't do this. He is faithful to His promise to His Son and to us to forgive us when we sin.

What does this verse mean when it says, "He is faithful and just to forgive us"? To be just is to be fair. Is it really fair to God to forgive us no matter what sins we have committed? Don't we have to be good enough to be saved?

No, I hope this is very clear to you by now—no one is

2. Psalm 50:15 NKJV
3. 1 John 1:9 NKJV

good enough to claim a right to heaven. Christ died for us to make us good in the sight of God. Because of what Christ did for us in dying on the cross and rising again from the dead, God has taken away all our guilt. The Scriptures declare, "As far as the east is from the west, so far has He removed our transgressions from us."[4]

Though we had no right whatever, Christ has made a road to heaven for us, and He takes us with Him right into the throne room of God, right into His holy presence. There Christ presents each of us to His Father as a new child of God, as Christ's new brother or sister. God welcomes us with warmth and excitement and joy as new members of His family.

Restoration

When we sin, we sadden God's heart, but when we confess our sins and turn away from them, we receive abundant forgiveness and restoration from God. The sins are cleansed away by the death of Christ. It is perfectly fair for God to forgive us because of what Christ has done in paying our penalty.

Well then, can we just go on sinning? Of course not! We want to please God, not displease Him with sin. If you aren't concerned about disobeying God, and don't care if you are hurting Him, then you need to check to see if you really do have Jesus in your life—if you really have accepted God's gift of forgiveness and salvation.

Remember, though, that the new life has not only a beginning but also growth. As you spend time with God you will want to please Him more and more, and you will

---

4. Psalm 103:12 NKJV

hate your sin, pride, and self-centeredness in whatever form it takes. You will see some good changes taking place in your life.

There will be less anger, more joy and peace; less lust and more genuine love for others; less lying and more stability and fearlessness. In short, your entire character will change for the better because now God's Holy Spirit is controlling your life and bringing in love, joy, patience, and all those other good things.

Let me repeat it: When you confess your sins to Him, He is faithful and just to forgive your sins, and to cleanse you from all impurity.

Taking Inventory

I strongly suggest that you stop now, take a sheet of paper and list those things in your life that need to be forgiven—things displeasing your Heavenly Father.

Is there bitterness? Refusal to forgive someone? Lust? Impurity? Cheating? Stealing?

List them all and take them to the Lord in prayer. Ask Him to forgive you and to help you concerning each item on your list.

Chapter Six

Your ears shall hear a word behind you, saying, "This is the way, walk in it," whenever you turn to the right hand or whenever you turn to the left.

Isaiah 30:21 NKJV

The Power of the Word of God

If you have ever planted a garden or watched your mother care for her potted plants you know how much care it takes to protect a young plant. You are a tender plant in God's garden, and you need a lot of nourishment and care. Otherwise you can become yellow and sickly and stunted—far from what God wants you to be and far from the happiness He intends you to have.

The difference between you and a young plant in a garden is that God insists that you take the initiative in the growth process. In a garden someone else tends the plants, and they simply grow. But in the Christian life, you must do certain things. God will help you, but He won't cause you to grow without your cooperation. God provides instructions; you must learn and apply them.

Reading the Bible

"When all else fails, read the instructions" is a funny but true statement. God has given us a whole Book of instructions that tells us how to please Him. This instruction manual is the Bible, and it is filled with nurture and vitamins for Christians new and old.

"The whole Bible was given to us by inspiration from God and is useful to teach us what is true and to make us realize what is wrong in our lives; it straightens us out and helps us do what is right."[1] This treasure trove is given to you by God, so one of the first actions of your new life must be to read the Bible. I suggest you plan to read it through at least once a year for the rest of your life. This will take ten minutes a day (out of the thousand minutes a day of your waking hours!). Additional time should be spent studying Bible themes or topics in order to familiarize yourself with all that the Bible says on certain subjects.

It is amazing to realize what good things will happen in your own life simply from reading the Bible and following its instructions.

Do you want happiness? Here is the way to get it: "Happy are all who perfectly follow the laws of God."[2] The Bible tells us what God wants us to do. Then, when we obey, happiness pours into our souls.

Do you want purity? "How can a young man stay pure? By reading your Word and following its rules."[3] The Holy Spirit gives us power to resist the strongest lusts, to walk away from temptation, and even to control and purify the thought life: It is the Holy Spirit's sharp scalpel that He uses to cut away the deep infections of sin, so that He can pour in the spiritual ointments that cause healing and joy. "I have thought much about your words, and stored

1. 2 Timothy 3:16 TLB
2. Psalm 119:1 TLB
3. Psalm 119:9 TLB

them in my heart so that they would hold me back from sin."[4]

Do you need a map for your life? Do you want something to show you where to go and how to get there? "Open my eyes to see wonderful things in your Word. I am but a pilgrim here on earth: how I need a map—and your commands are my chart and guide."[5] The Bible lays out principles that, if followed, are the strong foundation for life. A life founded on those principles will be a success in God's eyes and will be eternally rewarded. One of those principles is that right is right and wrong is wrong. Whatever the cost, do what is right and God will be pleased and honor you with His personal "Well done."

Others may flout God's law and achieve fame and fortune, and you probably could do the same. Yet that is not the path for you. He may or may not give you the good things of this life. He may call you to a steady walk in obscurity, but He will be with you, blessing you all the way.

Are you discouraged? You can be encouraged by reading the Bible: "I am completely discouraged—I lie in the dust. Revive me by your Word...encourage and cheer me with your words."[6] God's words will help you learn to cope with your daily trials.

Are you at heart a materialist? Do you long for "the good life"? Here is God's word for you on that subject: "Help me to prefer obedience to making money!"[7]

Do you need more faith? Who can overstate the importance of faith? Faith can move your mountains! Jesus said,

4. Psalm 119:11 TLB
5. Psalm 119:18,19 TLB
6. Psalm 119:25,28 TLB
7. Psalm 119:36 TLB

"If you had faith even as small as a tiny mustard seed you could say to this mountain, 'Move!' and it would go far away. Nothing would be impossible."[8]

Discovering What God Wants

The sword of God's Holy Spirit is the Bible, the Word of God. When the Holy Spirit goes into action in your life, more than dust flies! Your bad thoughts come under control, your bad actions wither and decline, and all the good things within you flourish and blossom. Good intentions that were never put into effect can now become a way of life. Bad habits you couldn't conquer come under the knife of the Master Surgeon.

All this from Bible reading? Yes, but there is one vital factor I haven't mentioned: Read to discover what God wants you to do, *and do it.* Those who read the Bible as (somewhat) interesting literature will not find it very exciting; those who read it as God's guidebook for their lives will find it to be a fascinating adventure.

What you need to do is to stop your Bible reading at the end of a paragraph or section or chapter and ask yourself and God: What can I learn from what I've just read about how You operate the world and about my life? Is there a lesson here for me? Can I find a spiritual principle here that answers a question I've had? (It's a good idea to keep a notebook with dates, jotting down what you learned each day.)

All right—incredible changes can and will occur in our outlook, our in-look, our attitudes toward God and others, as we read the Bible. But this is not a mysterious or

8. Matthew 17:20 TLB

mystical experience. It occurs simply because the Bible is God's Word. The Bible is "the sword of the Spirit" that cuts deep into our lives, opening the festering spiritual sores so that the healing of the Spirit can occur. Thus new life grows and flourishes.

Finding a Quiet Time

Then what should we do? Read the Bible regularly and thoughtfully, of course. I stress the great importance of finding a regular time for your daily "quiet time" to be with God: a time for Bible reading and prayer.

You will need to set a time and place for your reading (and your prayer time too, which I'll mention later). Many people do this when they first get up in the morning; others find it is more convenient after supper or at bedtime. I suggest that you stop right now as you are reading this and decide when you will have your daily Bible reading time. Also choose a quiet place where you can concentrate without undue interruption, if possible.

Now let me tell you a secret I've learned from years of experience as a Christian: Sometimes it takes a lot of self-discipline to read the Bible. You may tell yourself there just isn't time. I hope this won't be true in your case, but if it is, read on! If you find you are too busy to read God's instructions, and to give the Holy Spirit opportunity to bless you, then you are much too busy. The first thing to do is to cut back on TV, sports, reading, studying, or whatever—no matter how enjoyable or necessary your activity may seem—and spend time with God.

How much time should you spend daily? I don't know. There are too many variables in each individual's life that make it impractical for me to suggest more than a starting point. In my opinion an absolute minimum is to read the

Bible through each year, and to accomplish that, you will need about ten minutes a day. That is a minimum, certainly, for letting the Holy Spirit train what is His—meaning *you*—to become all He wants you to be.

Believing the Evidence

The Bible is God's message to mankind. In it He tells us what He wants us to be and to do. But other religions firmly believe that their sacred writings contain God's truth too. The Veda of the Hindus, the Koran of the Muslims, the Book of Mormon—all are trusted by millions. Why can we believe the claims of the Bible to be God's Word, as contrasted with all other such claims? Consider the following facts:

Fulfilled Prophecy Validates the Bible's Reliability

The Bible shows its reliability by relating coming events hundreds of years before they occurred.

Prophecy:

The prophet Micah—715 years before Christ was born in Bethlehem—wrote,

> O Bethlehem...you are but a small Judean village, yet you will be the birthplace of my King who is alive from everlasting ages past![9]

Fulfillment:

Jesus was born in the town of Bethlehem, in Judea, during the reign of King Herod. At about that time some astrologers from eastern lands arrived in Jerusalem, asking, "Where is the newborn King of the Jews? for we have seen his star in far-off eastern lands, and have come to worship

9. Micah 5:2 TLB

46

him." King Herod was deeply disturbed by their question, and all Jerusalem was filled with rumors. He called a meeting of the Jewish religious leaders. "Did the prophets tell us where the Messiah would be born?" he asked. "Yes, in Bethlehem," they said, "for this is what the prophet Micah wrote: 'O little town of Bethlehem, you are not just an unimportant Judean village, for a Governor shall rise from you to rule my people Israel.' "[10]

Prophecy:

The prophet Hosea wrote the following message 730 years before Christ was born,

When Israel was a child I loved him as a son and brought him out of Egypt.[11]

Fulfillment:

An angel of the Lord appeared to Joseph in a dream. "Get up and flee to Egypt with the baby and his mother," the angel said, "and stay there until I tell you to return, for King Herod is going to try to kill the child." That same night he left for Egypt with Mary and the baby, and stayed there until King Herod's death. This fulfilled the prophet's prediction, "I have called my Son from Egypt."[12]

Scores of other Old Testament prophecies were fulfilled in the coming of Jesus:

Jesus, when talking with some of his disciples, told them, "You find it so hard to believe all that the prophets wrote in the Scriptures! Wasn't it clearly predicted by the prophets that the Messiah would have to suffer all these things before entering his time of glory?" Then Jesus quoted them passage after passage from the writings of the prophets, beginning with the book of Genesis and going

10. Matthew 2:1–6 TLB
11. Hosea 11:1 TLB
12. Matthew 2:13–15 TLB

right on through the Scriptures, explaining what the passages meant and what they said about himself.[13]

Other religions do not have fulfilled prophecies to help prove that their sacred writings and doctrines are from God and not made up out of people's imaginations.

The Resurrection of Jesus Validates the Bible

That Christ's resurrection happened can hardly be doubted by those who carefully study the evidence. The Scripture documents indicate that the disciples of Jesus saw Him many times after His death and burial, and they suffered intense persecution for testifying to this fact. It is worthwhile to consider whether men will face torture and death for what they know to be a lie. This is unreasonable psychologically. As to whether the Scripture documents upon which we base our knowledge of Christ's death and resurrection are reliable: Books are available to those who wish to examine the evidence for themselves.[14]

Changed Lives Validate the Bible

More important evidence that the Bible is true is seen in the changed lives that result from people believing its message. The fruits of the Spirit—love, joy, peace, long-suffering, gentleness, goodness, and faithfulness—are present in the lives of committed Christians. Probably you yourself know one or more friends whose lives have changed now that they believe. Perhaps such fruitfulness is already occurring in your own life. I hope so.

13. Luke 24:25–27 TLB

14. See F. F. Bruce's *New Testament Documents: Are They Reliable?* (Downers Grove, Ill.: InterVarsity Press, rev. 1960) and Alan Hayward's *God's Truth!* (Nashville: Thomas Nelson Publishers, 1983).

Answers to Prayer Validate the Bible

Still another proof that the Scriptures are true is the fact that prayers are answered. The Scriptures declare that this will happen, and it does.

This matter of prayer is so important that we will devote the entire next chapter to it.

Chapter Seven

"Call to Me, and I will answer you, and show you great and mighty things, which you do not know."

Jeremiah 33:3 NKJV

The Power of Prayer

Approaching the Incredible God

Prayer may be the least understood, yet most wonderful, event in a Christian's life. It is hard to realize how powerful prayer is. It's not just saying a few words—it is actually talking to the eternal God. He is the incredible God who created everything there is, and who is in control of the universe which is expanding at the rate of 186,000 miles a second in all directions every hour—forever.

This God is your Father because of His mercy and love for you. He is not far off from you, surrounded by angel guards and impenetrable and death-dealing fire and glory. You as His child can come right into His presence where He joyfully welcomes you because you have become His.

Here is the way the Bible discusses this wonderful fact:

> You have not had to stand face to face with terror, flaming fire, gloom, darkness and a terrible storm, as the Israelites did at Mount Sinai when God gave them his laws. For there was an awesome trumpet blast, and a voice with a message so terrible that the people begged God to stop speaking.

They staggered back under God's command that if even an animal touched the mountain it must die. Moses himself was so frightened at the sight that he shook with terrible fear. But you have come right up into Mount Zion, to the city of the living God, the heavenly Jerusalem, and to the gathering of countless happy angels; and to the church, composed of all those registered in heaven; and to God who is Judge of all; and to the spirits of the redeemed in heaven, already made perfect; and to Jesus himself, who has brought us his wonderful new agreement; and to the sprinkled blood which graciously forgives instead of crying out for vengeance as the blood of Abel did.[1]

God not only allows you to come into the throne room of heaven with your thanks, your praise and your petitions, but He also wants you to do this. He loves for you to come and have companionship with Him; to let Him be your Father and you be His child as you stay there in quiet fellowship. How much more is involved than just "saying prayers"! So, prayer is not just asking. A human friend or parent would not be happy if you never talked except when asking for something! Yet prayer certainly involves asking too. Jesus said, "And all things, whatever you ask in prayer, believing, you will receive."[2] He also stated, "If you ask anything in My name, I will do it."[3]

You can come to God because Jesus opened the way for you by dying for your sins. You have the full rights of a much-loved child of God—the right to come with Jesus to the throne of the eternal God. You come as His brother or sister, using His name. It is the password—though it need not always be repeated. It is well understood in heaven by all the angels of glory that you belong there and

1. Hebrews 12:18–24 TLB
2. Matthew 21:22 NKJV
3. John 14:14 NKJV

have full privileges. Claim your privileges! Our Lord rejoices when you do.

Our Adoption

The story is told about a king who saw a beggar boy who had somehow wandered onto the king's estate. The guards were dealing roughly with him, but the king said, "No, bring the child to me." Filled with terror, the trembling boy was dragged before the king, expecting quick death. Instead the king announced, "I am going to adopt this boy into my own family. He is now my child. Give him food and clothes and bring him to me so that I can talk with him and help him learn how to be a child of the king."

This is what has happened to you. You were lost, apart from God, with no hope for the future when God sent for you and adopted you into His own family, making you His very own child. How incredible! How impossible! But how true!

Your Father, the King of glory, has notified all His attendants that He will welcome you at any time, day or night. He wants you to come. You are not to be interfered with or kept from His presence. The only thing that prevents you from talking things over with your Heavenly Father is you, yourself.

Make Time to Pray

I am sorry to say that many of God's children find they "don't have time" to spend with the One who gave them eternal life and who wants to have fellowship with them. They are too busy watching television or whatever, and they miss the opportunity of bringing joy to the heart of God by spending time with Him.

What can I suggest to you as a new Christian that will help you to learn the discipline of taking time for God? It is much the same kind of suggestion I have already given you about reading your Bible.

Make time in your busy schedule for prayer by cutting back on your other activities. This may mean dropping a course you are taking at school, putting the TV in a closet, getting up earlier, or something equally radical. You will probably pray very little unless you decide to do it and follow through at a regular time and place, but you can pray at any time, day or night, and God will hear you.

Some people get down on their knees to pray, some people walk or jog, some people sit. It doesn't really make any difference to God, for the question is reverence in our hearts rather than in our position. Personally I like to spend the time on my knees, sometimes beside my bed or a chair; sometimes, especially on cold mornings before the house is warm, I like to kneel under the covers or lie there talking to God (but sometimes this lends itself to going back to sleep, and if I find this happening I get up and brave the cold!).

Prayer Subjects

What should we pray about? I have a rather lengthy prayer list of family, friends, problems, triumphs, and projects, and I write these onto three- by five-inch "prayer cards" that are easy to carry. Very often part of my prayer time is spent talking to the Lord about the things He brings to my mind—things that may or may not be on the list, or that He especially wants me to pray about that day. Sometimes I know why it is important to pray about it that day, and sometimes I don't; but I follow directions. Sometimes I write down the date I enter the request on the card, and then the date that the answer comes. This follow-up gives great encouragement and impetus to my prayer life. Don't forget to thank God when the answer comes.

How to Listen to God

Prayer should be a two-way communication. Since there is no voice of God speaking in the room, you need to learn how He speaks in the silence of your heart and mind. I believe this takes practice and experience. Ask God to help you to know His will. If a thought keeps returning to you, talk it over with others. Don't act hastily. Not every thought that pops into your head while you are praying is from God.

Sometimes when you are praying about a problem, the answer will suddenly occur to you, and you will wonder why you hadn't thought of it before. The reason is that you hadn't prayed about it before, or hadn't prayed about it enough, or it was not God's time to give you the answer until that moment. It is important, though, to bring the idea before the Lord to discover whether it really is from Him or whether it is your own idea.

How Long to Pray

How long should we pray? I don't know. I have found it true that when I pray little, my heart becomes cool toward the Lord, and answers to prayer don't come as frequently as when I pray more often. This is of course logical and scriptural. We are told to persist in prayer.

I will tell you my own experience. For many years I had a quiet time, presumably on a daily basis. I say *presumably* because often I would realize that I hadn't spent time that particular day or even the day before, and in fact it might have been several days since I had my last quiet time. I had become too busy, partly in Christian work.

Finally I got tough with myself. After several days of fearfully thinking about it, I decided actually to do what I felt was reasonable and to try to spend a longer time with the Lord. I hoped to succeed in spending about an hour a day in prayer apart from my Bible reading time.

I remember how frightening it was the first time I tried to spend such a long period in the presence of the Lord. It seemed as though I would quickly run out of things to pray about, so I had the book of Psalms open to help me, as well as a list of items needing prayer attention.

It was difficult at first; nevertheless I survived! And I believe God was pleased. Anyway, I know that I have had some amazing answers to prayer and these times with God have become enjoyable and something I look forward to from morning to morning, though I still have days when I "skip."

Results of Prayer

Now a word needs to be said about the time when we ask God for something and we don't seem to receive it. The Bible tells us several reasons why this happens. You see, God knows what is best for us, and many times the things we ask for would not be in our best interests. Sometimes we ask for candy, not realizing that the candy we are asking for has some poison in it.

Another reason we don't see immediate answers to our earnest prayers is because it is not God's time to answer them. We are told to be patient and keep praying.

Our lives are His, and we should live by His timetable. A father may be eager to give his child what the child is asking for, but he has something better in mind to give at a later time—something that would be less valued or less appropriate if given now. Many a young man or woman falls desperately in love but finds the prayer for a mate is not answered. Then later, after being married to a more suitable person, he or she is happy that God did not answer the urgent earlier prayer!

Be patient in your praying. Don't demand instant answers of God. You may be asking for something less than that with which He desires to bless you.

Be glad for all God is planning for you.[4]

Rest in the Lord; wait patiently for him to act.[5]

Be patient in trouble, and prayerful always.[6]

Pray all the time. Ask God for anything in line with the Holy Spirit's wishes. Plead with him, reminding him of your needs, and keep praying earnestly for all Christians everywhere.[7]

Don't worry about anything; instead, pray about everything; tell God your needs and don't forget to thank him for his answers.[8]

Don't be weary in prayer; keep at it; watch for God's answers and remember to be thankful when they come.[9]

Always keep on praying.[10]

Let me suggest that you stop right now where you are sitting and ask God to show you when and where to begin your daily prayer time. Be businesslike about it, for if you never make the basic decision to spend time in prayer,

4. Romans 12:12 TLB
5. Psalm 37:7 TLB
6. Romans 12:12 TLB
7. Ephesians 6:18 TLB
8. Philippians 4:6 TLB
9. Colossians 4:2 TLB
10. 1 Thessalonians 5:17 TLB

and never make the basic decision about when and where, it may be weeks, months—or never—before you get around to having a regular, daily *sufficient diet* of prayer and Bible reading and study.

Chapter Eight

For whatever is born of God overcomes the world. And this is the victory that has overcome the world—our faith.

1 John 5:4 NKJV

The Power of Faith

God wants you to trust Him, to have faith in His love for you and in His willingness and power to help you.

Men of God in days of old were famous for their faith.[1]

Without faith it is impossible to please Him.[2]

"If your faith were only the size of a mustard seed," Jesus answered, "it would be large enough to uproot that mulberry tree over there and send it hurtling into the sea! Your command would bring immediate results!"[3]

Why Have Faith?

Why does God want you to have more faith? Is it so you can become famous as a mountain-mover or an uprooter of trees? No, of course not! It is so you can pray more effectively for His church and serve Him more usefully by developing new strength and larger talents for His glory.

1. Hebrews 11:2 TLB
2. Hebrews 11:6 NKJV
3. Luke 17:6 TLB

How do we get that kind of faith? The Bible tells us, "Faith comes by hearing [or reading]...the word of God."[4]

I am sure that your experience will be like mine. As I read God's promises to His children, and see what miraculous things happen when His people pray, I am inspired to believing faith concerning matters about which I feel led to pray.

What a pleasure it is to God to have His children trusting Him, and how easily He can then respond. A great deal is said in our Handbook from Heaven (the Bible) about the fact that God answers our prayers more readily if we trust Him and believe that He is going to do what we pray for, if it is best.

If you are as serious as I believe you to be, you will begin at once to read the gospel accounts of miracles and ask God to increase your faith. Many times when my faith has been at a low ebb I have gone to the Gospels or to the book of Acts or to the stories of the Old Testament about mighty miracles. Each time my faith has grown. I have realized not only the power of God—that He is able to solve my problems and use me for His work—but also His willingness to do this.

Healing Faith

A wonderful biblical story tells about a man who brought his son to Jesus because the son was demon-possessed. The demon often dashed the child to the ground and knocked him unconscious so that he lay there foaming at the mouth and grinding his teeth.

4. Romans 10:17 NKJV

The father brought the boy to Jesus and when the evil spirit saw Jesus, it threw the boy into a convulsion.

Jesus asked the father, "How long has he been this way?"

The father replied, "Since he was very small. And the demon often makes him fall into the fire or into the water to kill him. Oh, have mercy on us and do something if you can."

Then Jesus said to him, "If I can? Anything is possible if you have faith."

Immediately the boy's father cried out, "I do have faith; oh, help me to have more!" Then Jesus commanded the evil spirit to come out of the boy and never to enter him again, and so the boy was healed.[5]

This true story shows us that the father realized his faith was not strong enough, so he asked the Lord Jesus to help him have more faith. As he saw his son healed, how that father's faith in Jesus' power and love must have grown.

So you see, in the end we depend on Jesus to give us more faith. He is willing to do this if we ask Him and if we follow His method by reading His Word, and praying for faith to believe.

The Faith Chapter

I need to caution you not to think that more faith means more money, health, fame, success, or other worldly goodies. In the famous Bible chapter about faith (see Hebrews 11), there is a deep contrast between the joyous results of faith for some and the persecution that

---

5. Mark 9:17–27 TLB

came to others. Yet all had the same faith and God was pleased with both.

> These people all trusted God and as a result won battles, overthrew kingdoms, ruled their people well, and received what God had promised them; they were kept from harm in a den of lions, and in a fiery furnace. Some, through their faith, escaped death by the sword. Some were made strong again after they had been weak or sick. Others were given great power in battle; they made whole armies turn and run away. And some women, through faith, received their loved ones back again from death. But others trusted God and were beaten to death, preferring to die rather than turn from God and be free—trusting that they would rise to a better life afterwards.
>
> Some were laughed at and their backs cut open with whips, and others were chained in dungeons. Some died by stoning and some by being sawed in two; others were promised freedom if they would renounce their faith, then were killed with the sword. Some went about in skins of sheep and goats, wandering over deserts and mountains, hiding in dens and caves. They were hungry and sick and ill-treated—too good for this world.[6]

Am I saying that sometimes the mountains don't move when we pray in faith? I am saying that God's purpose is achieved, and sometimes that purpose is to let us go through trouble for His glory.

What about Suffering?

Sometimes God allows us to enter into Christ's sufferings. The Apostle Paul writes about his own suffering:

> We are in deep trouble for bringing you God's comfort and salvation. But in our trouble God has comforted us—and this, too, to help you: to show you from our personal

6. Hebrews 11:33–38 TLB

experience how God will tenderly comfort you when you undergo these same sufferings. He will give you the strength to endure.[7]

But part of my work is to suffer for you; and I am glad, for I am helping to finish up the remainder of Christ's sufferings for his body, the church.[8]

Now I have given up everything else—I have found it to be the only way to really know Christ and to experience the mighty power that brought him back to life again, and to find out what it means to suffer and to die with him. So, whatever it takes, I will be one who lives in the fresh newness of life of those who are alive from the dead.[9]

What a strange thing Paul is saying—that those men and women of faith who suffer instead of triumphing are equally in the will of God, and in some mysterious way they share a special fellowship of suffering along with their Savior.

Many stories of faith-filled missionaries don't end triumphantly from a human point of view. One of my vivid college memories is of a chapel service, with Peter Stam, Jr. at the organ. During the service he was handed a note which (we learned later) gave him news of the beheading of his brother John and John's wife in China by the invading Communist forces.

And I remember the time a few years later when the newspapers were filled with stories about the death of five young missionaries who went to the Auca Indian tribe in South America to preach the good news to them. But before they had that opportunity, they were speared to death by the Aucas. These missionaries were men of

7. 2 Corinthians 1:6,7 TLB
8. Colossians 1:24 TLB
9. Philippians 3:10,11 TLB

faith who moved mountains, but not as they had expected. Now, many years later, the tribe is filled with Christians as a result of those martyrs' deaths.

Trust and Obedience

However, most of us are called to strength, joy, and power through faith, not primarily to suffering. But whether God gives you pleasure or suffering, learn to trust and obey, and watch the good changes in your own life and in the lives of those around you. Know that God in heaven is filled with joy too, because you are trusting Him.

From my own experience I know that there are times when it is difficult to trust. I remember once when a fairly large sum of money was needed in an organization I am associated with, with serious consequences to befall us if we were unable to pay a certain bill by noon. Several of us met in my office and got down on our knees and prayed. We asked and even begged the Lord for His help, and while we were praying there was a knock on the door. Then someone handed me a note saying that the needed amount had just arrived from an unexpected source!

But sometimes, although I have prayed with faith, the answer has not come—yet. So I keep on praying, and God will answer in His own good time and way—or even tell me "no." And since I want God's will alone, that is all right with me, though sometimes not without a struggle. God's way for your life is the only good way, and I long for you to find and follow it all your days and nights forever.

PART THREE

Obeying
God's Commands

Chapter Nine

Above all else, guard your affections. For they influence everything else in your life.

Proverbs 4:23 TLB

Hindrances to the Christian

Jesus said, "If you love Me, keep My commandments."[1] How important it is, then, to know what it is He wants us to do, or doesn't want us to do. Yet even when we know, sometimes it seems so hard to obey. Why is this? After all He has done for us and all we want to do for Him, why is obedience so difficult? The Bible tells us why.

You and I and all of us—everyone, everywhere—are born with sinful tendencies. This is true because of a spiritual law we can't change: When sin entered the world, all became sinners. We each inherit a defective spiritual gene that makes us susceptible to sinning. Satan himself engineered this plan. God overcame it by forgiving our sins through what Christ did, but the genes are still there. Then God sent His Holy Spirit to overcome those genes by deadening their influence and causing their power to debilitate. We can overcome this tendency toward sin,

---

1. John 14:15 NKJV

unless we turn from the Holy Spirit's help and follow our own way again—then at once the old, evil spiritual genes become powerful again until we confess our sin and turn back to God's path.

Satan is not likely to let us go without a fight. Again and again he will tempt us to turn away from what is right. The Bible says he is like a roaring lion seeking stray sheep that have left their Shepherd's care. He can attack and capture them and lead them into sin and sorrow, until they wake up from their stupor and cry out to the Savior for help. Then Satan slinks away, waiting for another opportunity to pounce.

Let's examine some of Satan's devices to lead us astray.

Peer Pressure

Teenagers especially don't want to be different from their friends. They want to wear the "in" styles of haircuts and clothes, to drink, to do drugs and have sex—whatever their friends or heroes are doing.

For most non-Christians God's will is not a viable option, but for you as a new Christian at whatever age, His will is imperative. When He says one thing and your friends say another, then you must go your way with God and let your friends leave you if they wish. A simple choice, but resulting sometimes in deep changes in your life-style and companionship.

Permissive Sex

Let's face it—fornication and adultery are "acceptable" to the media decision makers. Every soap opera and most movies and novels carry the theme explicitly or implicitly, with approval. And if everybody is doing it, it's as easy for a Christian as for anyone else to be drawn into Satan's master plot of using a wonderful gift of God for his own evil purposes. Evil? Yes. Who says so? God does.

A prostitute is a dangerous trap; those cursed of God are caught in it.[2]

For the land is full of adultery and the curse of God is on it.[3]

You have had enough in the past of the evil things the godless enjoy—sex sin, lust, getting drunk, wild parties, drinking bouts.[4]

Homosexuality is absolutely forbidden.[5]

Wrong Time Use

Satan wants you to be too busy to have time for God. You need to study, you need to have some recreation, you need to rush here and there. All are good activities, but all are totally wrong if God doesn't have the top priority. How much time do you spend watching TV? How much time reading God's Word? How much time doing this and that? How much time in prayer? You see, it's your decision whether God comes first. Will you occasionally fit Him in with your other priorities, or does God set your priorities? I write this very matter of factly. Would that I could shout it in such a way that you would take it absolutely seriously, for it can make an eternal difference.

Materialism

Materialism means wanting money and all the good things it brings. Almost everyone aspires to a life of comfort and affluence—a new car, a fine home, new furni-

2. Proverbs 22:14 TLB
3. Jeremiah 23:10 TLB
4. 1 Peter 4:3 TLB
5. Leviticus 18:22 TLB

ture, and so on. God gives us the ability to have the job and the talent to work well and be promoted or get a raise. But we have to decide how to spend our money. If our goal is the good things of this life, that is what we will spend it on. But if we realize that all of our money (as well as time and talent) belongs to God, then our goal cannot be wealth unless we desire to give it to God. This is not always so easy; many rich Christians find it hard to part with their money.[6]

Hear the Word of God on this question: "Don't store up treasures here on earth where they can erode away or may be stolen. Store them in heaven where they will never lose their value, and are safe from thieves. If your profits are in heaven your heart will be there too."[7]

Pride

Pride comes before a fall. This adage, based on Scripture, is certainly true of spiritual growth. Pride of status, wealth, athletic or intellectual ability (or both), pride of physique or beauty, or business ability, or car, or fine home—all are false. Whatever privileges or abilities you have are from God, so why act as though you had done some great thing? Instead, humbly thank God and put all your God-given abilities and resources under His direction. Pride is self-worship, and God will not honor it with the greening of your spirit or the power and fruit of His Holy Spirit in your life.

Sin

Sin is a wide-ranging word. It means thinking and act-

6. See Matthew 25:14–29 TLB
7. Matthew 6:19–21 TLB

ing contrary to God's will. None of us is free from these failures, and a spiritual deficit always results. Daily confession of sin, turning from it and being forgiven, is a constant necessity for a fruitful, God-pleasing life. Don't wait for your next quiet time with God to make things right with Him. When the evil thought or sin occurs, confess it right away.

As we have discussed, we have an inherited disposition to sin, and Satan takes full advantage of this fact. If we are not on guard, he can lure us into temptation and into sin. A daily time of Bible reading and prayer is a primary means of defeating Satan's power.

And what about when we do sin? God is ready to forgive us: "But if we confess our sins to him, he can be depended on to forgive us and to cleanse us from every wrong."[8]

Discouragement and Depression

Discouragement is a powerful enemy to joy and peace, which are among the fruits of the Spirit. Discouragement harms us spiritually, and therefore Satan uses it as often as he can to fell us.

What is the cause of discouragement? If you look closely at it, you will see that it usually comes as the result of a failure to attain something you want. Several possible solutions will help you overcome it, but the most important one is to discover if what you want is what God wants or if it is merely your own desire. I have friends who insist on this or that career, or other objectives (I've done this myself) either without consulting God or

---

8. 1 John 1:9 TLB

71

going ahead despite the obvious warnings. In mercy, God sometimes intervenes and allows failure. Take courage. Follow God out of the swamp and back onto His personal pathway for you. God's goals for you may not be what you had in mind, but in choosing His way you will have joy, peace, and contentment.

Then, of course, you may experience well-deserved discouragement with yourself because you have messed up. Again the solution is to ask God to rebuild your life and to give you courage and strength to stay with the task.

There are times, too, when discouragement is simply due to weariness. The solution may be to get more sleep or to reduce your activities to better suit your strength.

Tribulation

The Apostle Paul went through discouraging times that didn't get him down. He was in prison for several years at various times because he broke the law by preaching about Christ. Yet God comforted him, and he was able to comfort and encourage others as a result. The Christian life is not always just a bed of roses. There are briars and thorns along with the flowers. God has not promised skies that stay blue. But He has promised to be with us in times of trouble, if we will let Him. Our trust isn't for deliverance, but for His presence and power within, even when He allows difficulty and tragedy.

Opposition from Family or Friends

This is a tough one, and when Satan uses it, he uses it to the hilt. It's no fun to be scorned and laughed at by friends and those you love. But sometimes it happens.

Jesus said, "A man's worst enemies will be right in his own home!"[9]

Jesus also said of His disciples (including you): "Anyone who obeys my Father in heaven is my brother, sister and mother!"[10] Keep on loving those opposing you and Satan will be put to shame as the love of Jesus fills your life.

Unbelief and Doubting

Even those who love the Lord are attacked by Satan when he brings up the question: "Can all this really be true?" That is how he tempted Eve in the Garden of Eden:

> The serpent was the craftiest of all the creatures the Lord God had made. So the serpent came to the woman. "Really?" he asked. "*None* of the fruit in the garden? God says you mustn't eat *any* of it?"
>
> "Of course we may eat it," the woman told him. "It's only the fruit from the tree at the *center* of the garden that we are not to eat. God says we mustn't eat it or even touch it, or we will die."
>
> "That's a lie!" the serpent hissed. "You'll not die! God knows very well that the instant you eat it you will become like him, for your eyes will be opened—you will be able to distinguish good from evil!"[11]

And Satan still uses this technique that worked so successfully:

"Is He a God of love? Then why is there so much poverty and disaster?"

9. Matthew 10:36 TLB
10. Matthew 12:50 TLB
11. Genesis 3:1–5 TLB

"The Bible and science don't agree."

"You have sinned too much to be forgiven."

"You've done it again. How many times do you expect God to forgive you?"

"Your professor is a wise man—and he doesn't believe."

These and other similar remarks work to Satan's benefit by raising doubts and encouraging unbelief. It is certainly true that we cannot answer some of the questions Satan asks—though many of them we can. Take the questions to the Lord. Keep open the lines of communication. Continue your study of the Christian Life Handbook (the Bible). Trust God and move onward—with Him.

An interesting story in the Old Testament tells about a battle between the Israelites and the Amalekites. Joshua was the captain of the Israeli army; but Moses, an old man by now, stood on a hill watching the battle. At God's command, when he kept his arm stretched out, the Israelites prevailed; but when his arms became tired and he let them down to rest, the Amalekites began winning. So two of Moses' assistants held up his arms and the Israelites won the battle.

This principle can be easily applied to the Christian and his battle against Satan. If you stand firm with your heart lifted up to heaven, asking God's help against the army of Satan, the Holy Spirit is able to defeat Satan. If, however, you try to win the battle by yourself, your defeat is inevitable. That is why it is so important to spend time every day in personal communication with your Commander-in-Chief in heaven, the Lord Jesus Christ, asking Him to send the Holy Spirit afresh into your life each day. Then the temptations, called in Scripture "the fiery darts of the wicked one,"[12] are turned aside by the shield of salvation, and Satan is attacked and defeated by the "sword of the Spirit—which is the Word of God."[13]

Now that I have sketched the general background of success against Satan, here are some specifics. We are told to "resist the devil and he will flee from you"[14] and to "make no provision for the flesh, to fulfill its lusts."[15]

It is easily possible for you to get yourself into situations in which you walk right into Satan's den. Some examples might include getting into the back seat of the car, walking past an X-rated movie theater, sitting next to a person who is willing to assist you with answers to an exam.

Bitterness and Unforgiveness

God is love, and His children are to love, not hate. He has forgiven us, and we must forgive others. If we refuse to forgive them, will God forgive us? The Bible has some serious warnings about this.

How are we to forgive someone who has wronged us, perhaps devastated us, even destroyed us? There is no way we can do it by ourselves. Only God the Holy Spirit within us can give us the desire and the strength.

Give us the desire to forgive? Yes, that's the first giant step. We want our enemy to suffer from our unforgiveness, not realizing that he (or she) doesn't really care, and

12. Ephesians 6:16b NKJV
13. Ephesians 6:17b TLB
14. James 4:7 TLB
15. Romans 13:14 NKJV

we are only torturing ourselves. We try to cling to our anger. But God says no. That is not for us. Jesus said, "Love your enemies."[16]

The Apostle John said, "He who dislikes his brother is wandering in spiritual darkness and doesn't know where he is going, for the darkness had made him blind so that he cannot see the way."[17] This is a strong statement. It means that if we refuse to forgive, we need to ask ourselves if we are really Christians at all.

Notice that I said, "If we refuse to forgive." When each of us reaches the point of saying to God, "I know I *must* forgive, *help me* to forgive," then the Holy Spirit is able to open that closed, stinking room of our hearts and cleanse it by helping us truly forgive. Only then can we begin to show brotherly or sisterly affection, learning to love that person who hurt us, and long for him or her to experience God's healing too.

In this way Satan is doubly defeated and God is glorified; the poison is drained from our lives and replaced with all that is good. Even non-Christian psychologists tell us that one of the great penalties we pay for not forgiving others is living in bitterness. Jesus told His disciples to forgive "seventy times seven!"[18]

However, forgiveness is more than an act of the will; it is also an emotion. Whether the other person deserves it or not, and whether we feel like it or not—we must decide, with God's help, to forgive. Then, having decided to forgive, the healing process can begin, the bitterness can start to wilt, and the root of bitterness will itself die away.

16. Matthew 5:44; Luke 6:27 TLB
17. 1 John 2:11 TLB
18. Matthew 18:22 TLB

Sometimes this is a lengthy process, but forgiveness is vital for our own sakes and before God, who said that He would not forgive us if we would not forgive those who have sinned against us. All sorts of physical and emotional sicknesses that can begin with the trauma of unforgiveness can be healed by the process of forgiving.

Sometimes the hardest person to forgive may be yourself. "Oh, why did I do such a foolish thing? Oh, that I had done it this or that way instead. Oh, that I had not given way and committed the sin. Oh, that I had not said that word or done that wrong that has irreparably changed my life. And I can never go back to that point; I must always have second best."

The fact is that you need to commit the past to your Savior and go forward into the glorious present and future He has for you. It can be fully wonderful; spending time in remorse for the past ways you have hurt yourself and others is unprofitable. Make right whatever you can at whatever the cost, and then ask God to help you forgive yourself and go on to the joy and power He will give you, hand in hand with Him, under His fresh blessing.

To forgive one who has wronged you is truly a divine act, but it is essential. If you who have been forgiven refuse to forgive, how can you say that you are a lover of the Lord and yet disobey His primary command to love?

I find that it helps to pray for the person who has hurt me. I don't know what his or her inner struggles are, but my prayer help as a fellow Christian is doubtless needed. Your prayers will erode the dam that has kept you distant from the person who hurt you, until finally one day you will find that you truly have forgiven that person.

Chapter Ten

I would have you learn this great fact: that a life of doing right is the wisest life there is.

Proverbs 4:11 TLB

Life-Style

Now that you believe, you may need to radically change your life-style. If fornication has been in your life-style, or cheating or lying or gossiping, you must stop all these harmful actions. With God's help through your new life in Christ, by the power of the Holy Spirit, you will be able to stop them. There is no place for these things in the will of God.

How to Change

How in the world can you suddenly stop sins and wrong habits that have gripped your life, perhaps for a long time? The answer lies in the fact that Satan is no longer your master; he has lost control of your life. You belong to Christ, and He lives in you now. Satan can still tempt you, but in Christ's power you can say no and walk away from the temptation. The Holy Spirit is now in your heart to help you.

All by itself, our determination to do right just doesn't seem to work, for we are fighting against Satan's power.

He entices us to do wrong, and he is too strong for us to stand against—unless we have God's help.

God's help is what God gives us when we become His children. He plants the Holy Spirit within us, and we can ask the Spirit to send Satan's power reeling into the corner.

The most important thing to remember is that you can't be what you want to be and what God wants you to be without the Holy Spirit's help. What you want to be is kind, good, loving, strong, and fearless. These qualities are the results of the Spirit living in you.

It has been well said that if you plant a thought, you reap an action. Plant an action and reap a habit. Plant a habit and reap a character. It all begins with the thought life, and who can wrest the thought life from Satan's wiles except the Spirit of God?

The Holy Spirit now lives within you and is willing to take over and make you the person you have always wanted to be—the one God expects you to be. Yet He can't do it unless you let Him. No wonder we are told, "Don't you realize that you can choose your own master?...Thank God that though you once chose to be slaves of sin, now you have obeyed with all your heart the teaching to which God has committed you."[1]

But don't expect the Holy Spirit to transform you if you refuse to let Him have all of you to work with. "I plead with you to give your bodies to God. Let them be a living sacrifice, holy—the kind he can accept. When you

---

1. Romans 6:16,17 TLB

think of what he has done for you, is this too much to ask?"[2]

If you are holding back part of yourself from Him, you are limiting His power in your life. How much of you does He have? Who really runs your life?

The answers to these questions are vitally important. The first business at hand after you become a Christian is to turn yourself over to Him. If you have not given Him all of yourself and your life, then now is the time. Don't let this matter wait for "later on." "Later on" may never come. You may become more and more hardened to His call and never yield yourself completely to Him.

I talked to a man the other day who was well dressed and looked the part of a successful businessman. I asked him what his work was, and he told me he was unemployed. His response surprised me, and I asked him where he had worked before and what had happened. Did the business go bankrupt or what? No, he said, the business was doing very well. He was the treasurer of a company and was instructed to hide some financial transactions so that his company could avoid some taxes. He refused, and he was fired.

Now that you are a Christian you will have many opportunities to betray your Lord by accepting peer pressure to do wrong. It may be that in the past you surrendered and went along with the crowd. But now you are a brand new creature and have no right to sin. Sometimes, perhaps often, you will have to stand alone against the crowd. You may find that your friends desert you and laugh at you and you will have to find new

2. Romans 12:1 TLB

friends. "Of course, your former friends will be very surprised when you don't eagerly join them any more in the wicked things they do, and they will laugh at you in contempt and scorn."[3]

This course of action may be painful for you, but in many cases it is necessary; otherwise you may be led back into the old paths of compromise and sin. When you were a viper, other vipers didn't attack you; but now that you are a man or woman of God, they will. Get out of the vipers' nest and walk alone if you need to until you can find your place of fellowship among God's people.

God's Temple

You are God's holy temple. God is in you. If He is not, then you are not a Christian at all. Since the Holy God is in you, you must always strive for holiness too.

He has already forgiven your sins of the past, and He will continue to forgive you when you, as His child, sin. But if you sin deliberately and continuously, you need to ask yourself seriously if you are really a Christian at all. If you are, then you must seek to please Him in all you say, think, and do.

All forms of sexual sin—fornication, adultery, and so on—are strictly taboo. God says so: "Don't spend your time in wild parties and getting drunk or in adultery and lust, or fighting, or jealousy. But ask the Lord Jesus Christ to help you live as you should, and don't make plans to enjoy evil."[4] Heavy petting is surely taboo too, for who can avoid mental fornication under such circum-

---

3. 1 Peter 4:4 TLB
4. Romans 13:12b–14 TLB

stances? Christ has strictly prohibited lust as being the same as the sin itself, *and it is sin*. Keep away from it.

So learn to flee youthful lusts.[5] Make no provision for permitting it—seducing or being seduced. Is this too much to bear? Of course not! The Lord Jesus Christ and His Holy Spirit will help you if you do your part. You are not an automaton, driven by your lust and desires. You can resist the devil, and he will flee from you.

What Are My Limits?

Here is a brief survey of major Scripture themes on Christian life-style:

The Ten Commandments [6]

1., 2. *Never worship any other god*. This rules out not only heathen idols but current heroes. It means giving up the worship of money and all it can buy, as well as the longing for popularity or fame—which is self-worship.

3. *No swearing*. God's name is holy. Should you drag it in the mud? Similar prohibitions forbid foul talk of every kind. "Dirty stories, foul talk and coarse jokes—these are not for you. Instead, remind each other of God's goodness and be thankful."[7]

4. *Remember to observe the Sabbath as a holy day*. Although this injunction is not as restrictive in the New Testament as in the Old Testament, before Christ came, the principle remains that God wants His people to have a day of rest from their usual routines.

5. *Honor your father and mother*. Good things happen as a result. The Bible says: "Honor your father and mother.

---

5. See 2 Timothy 2:22 TLB
6. See Exodus 20:1–17 TLB
7. Ephesians 5:4 TLB

This is the first of God's Ten Commandments that ends with a promise."[8]

6. *Don't murder.* (In my opinion this commandment clearly applies to killing the unborn.)

7. *No adultery, fornication, or other sexual sins.* Sex is wonderful in its proper place—within marriage—but a savage destroyer outside. Avoid it like the plague—not because of fear of disease or other consequences, but because God your Heavenly Father absolutely prohibits it.

8. *No stealing.* (That includes cheating.)

9. *No lying.*

10. *Don't covet.* Proper ambition and goals are good, but be content with what God gives you.

Christ's Summary of the Law

I used to wonder how to remember all the commandments of God. As a child I memorized the Ten Commandments in the Bible, but there are so many other commandments in the Bible—hundreds of them. Then I discovered a wonderful fact, that the first and greatest commandment is to love God. We read about it in the Scriptures where a lawyer asked Jesus,

"Which is the most important command in the laws of Moses?"

Jesus replied, " 'Love the Lord your God with all your heart, soul, and mind.' This is the first and greatest commandment. The second most important is similar: 'Love your neighbor as much as you love yourself.' All the other commandments and all the demands of the prophets stem from these two laws and are fulfilled if you obey them.

8. Ephesians 6:2 TLB

Keep only these and you will find that you are obeying all the others.'"⁹

So it isn't as complicated as I had thought! Love God completely, and do to your neighbor as you, in your best moments, want him or her to do to you. If we obey only these two basic laws, we will be obeying all the others, too.

It is wonderful of God to tell us what He allows and what He prohibits, what He likes and dislikes, for we might otherwise be unsure of ourselves, and unsure whether or not we are loving God by obeying Him. Here are some more of His rules.

Other Rules

- *Drunkenness* is prohibited. Beer busts may be fun at the moment, but they are not God's way for you.
- *Homosexuality* and *bestiality* are absolutely forbidden.
- *Drugs* damage your body, which is the sacred temple of God. The dangers of alcohol are often mentioned in the Bible. And even though drugs like pot and cocaine are not mentioned, it is clear why you shouldn't violate yourself with substances that produce physical, mental, and often severe moral damage.

The Positives

Now let's look at another category of elements—the good things God desires for you. Here are some of them:

- *Love* for God and people.

9. Matthew 22:36–40 TLB

- *Power* in prayer.
- *Joy* of the Lord.
- *Fearlessness*. Forget your timidity—God will help you overcome it.
- *Humility*. See yourself as God's much-loved child—gifted in many ways—and undeserving. The abilities and talents you have are God-given, so why be proud as though you were a self-made person?
- *Patience*. God wants you to have it. Ask Him for it.
- *Gentleness*. Same as above!
- *Guilelessness*. Purity of heart. Genuineness. These are all aspects of the character God desires for you.
- *Strength* in the Lord. Fearlessness against peer pressure. Willing to take a stand for righteousness.

Questionables

Still another category of actions and attitudes is not mentioned in Scripture, and Christians have various viewpoints about whether they are right or wrong. These include such things as the use of tobacco, social drinking, movies, ballroom dancing, rock music, and so on.

There are those who believe that these actions are allowed, and those who don't think they are appropriate. The Apostle Paul speaks at length about a problem of this nature in the church in Rome, where some thought there was no harm in buying and eating meat that had been offered as sacrifices to idols, but others felt it was a terrible thing to do because it made them partakers in idol worship. The apostle, after carefully showing both points of view, says that this is something each person can decide for himself.

However—and this is a huge qualification—the apostle says that if you are with a Christian brother or sister who abhors eating such food, you shouldn't do it. This act would be offensive and therefore unloving. Showing loving consideration for the other person's feelings is much more important than having your own way. Paul declares that for himself, although he has no objection to eating such meat, he won't do it (or drink wine, he adds) if this would cause someone to stumble. "Why injure the kingdom of God for a chunk of meat?" he asks.[10]

The pros and cons of today's differences of opinion are easy to list. Movies occasionally are thought-provoking, but usually filled with sex, violence, and profound godlessness that inevitably affects our own attitudes. "Garbage in, garbage out" applies to what we feed our souls. "Liquor is pleasant," say those who indulge. "Liquor is terribly dangerous—one in ten will die a drunkard's death after God dishonoring, wasted years and the destruction of your family," say those who don't drink. Gambling is recreation, say those who do. "It is addictive for many and economically disastrous," say those who don't.

Use your best and prayerful judgment, well salted with Scripture, when deciding whether to do debatable things that are not clearly prohibited by God. And when you see others doing things you feel they shouldn't—things not prohibited in the Scriptures—try not to be offended, but proceed, carefully following your own convictions. "Give a warm welcome to any brother who wants to join you, even though his faith is weak. Don't criticize him for having different ideas from yours about what is right and wrong."[11] If others are offended by the stand you take,

---

10. See Romans 14 and 15 TLB
11. Romans 14:1 TLB

carefully consider giving up your rights in favor of not offending them.

It is all a matter of *balance*—not going overboard in either direction. I am sure that there are times when it is impractical and illogical to avoid offending someone by your actions that are in the "gray area" where the Lord has not indicated in the Scriptures what is right and wrong. Let your purpose be to give as little offense as possible while moving steadily forward with the Lord.

What to Do When Temptations Come

That temptations will come is guaranteed! Satan is mad about your escaping his net, and although there is always a way of escape, he keeps trying to snare you back into the darkness, hoping you won't find the way out again, or that you will forget where it is.

But remember this—the wrong desires that come into your life aren't anything new and different. Many others have faced exactly the same problems before you. And no temptation is irresistible. You can trust God to keep the temptation from becoming so strong that you can't stand up against it, for he has promised this and will do what he says. He will show you how to escape temptation's power so that you can bear up patiently against it.[12]

Even if we believe that it makes no difference to the Lord whether we do these things, still we cannot just go ahead and do them to please ourselves; for we must bear the "burden" of being considerate of the doubts and fears of others—of those who feel these things are wrong. Let's please the other fellow, not ourselves, and do what is for his good and thus build him up in the Lord.[13]

12. 1 Corinthians 10:13 TLB
13. Romans 15:1,2 TLB

This is the law of love. But, you may well say, others are also supposed to be tolerant of me. That is true; but if they aren't, then the law of love says to submit to the "injustice" of their failure and give up the smoking (or whatever the bone of contention is), or shift to a church fellowship where this is not a problem.

An Example

Just recently I talked with a young woman—let's call her "Susie"—whose story is fairly common. Brought up in a staunch Christian home, she thinks she accepted the Lord when she was a child. But for some reason she never particularly grew and matured as a Christian. She experienced no joy or peace and had a great deal of depression from time to time.

She didn't go to college, but eventually found a job in a warehouse. She worked there for several years before quitting. Then she went to California and got into the drug and alcohol scene. Eventually she returned home again and lived with her parents, successfully concealing her problems—except that she was obviously very unhappy.

A former friend of hers, who had been as unhappy as she was, became a happy Christian. He and his wife invited Susie to visit them for a couple of weeks and she did. While she was with them she began to see the light of day and some hope. She realized that her problem was based on the fact that she had never really been a Christian at all; or if she was, she certainly wasn't letting Christ control her life and give her happiness. So as best as she could she turned her life over to God. From that time forward she began to be somewhat happy and somewhat pleasant. Susie began to grow and to flower as the Holy

Spirit was able more and more to tenderize, water, and nurture the seeds of life planted in her heart.

Now she is beginning to go to church and enjoy it. As a member of the singles group in the church, she is beginning to develop some new friends. Part of her problem at first was that she was trying to avoid the former friends who had been so unhelpful to her before she had replaced them with new friendships.

However, from time to time, and much to her own disgust, Susie still gets depressed and discouraged. And she goes on an occasional alcoholic binge.

I asked Susie about the time she spends daily with God in Bible reading and prayer. She answered that she had no regular plan of action. That's where Susie is making her mistake. She isn't taking advantage of the armor provided by God to all of His children. It isn't surprising that she gets depressed and discouraged. She is trying to fight Satan's attacks alone.

The Word of God is the sword of the Spirit and the shield of faith. The Word of God protects against and quenches the fiery arrows launched at close range by Satan. Use it!

Chapter Eleven

And when the Chief Shepherd appears, you will receive the crown of glory that does not fade away.

1 Peter 5:4 NKJV

Jesus Is Coming Back

Why do I mention in a book for new Christians the fact that Jesus is coming back? Because I think it is the greatest event of the future and it may happen soon. Most people never give it a thought, but when Jesus left for heaven, He told the disciples that He would return. Concerning this event, the Apostle Paul both warns and encourages us to be ready and waiting. We read in the book of Acts about Jesus leaving:

> It was not long afterwards that he rose into the sky and disappeared into a cloud, leaving them [his disciples] staring after him. As they were straining their eyes for another glimpse, suddenly two white-robed men were standing there among them, and said, ''Men of Galilee, why are you standing here staring at the sky? Jesus has gone away to heaven, and some day, just as he went, he will return!''[1]

The Apostle Paul tells us more about it:

And so I would say to you who are suffering, God will give you rest along with us when the Lord Jesus appears sud-

1. Acts 1:9–11 TLB

denly from heaven in flaming fire with his mighty angels, bringing judgment on those who do not wish to know God, and who refuse to accept his plan to save them through our Lord Jesus Christ.[2]

The Apostle also tells us:

But I am telling you this strange and wonderful secret: we shall not all die, but we shall all be given new bodies! It will all happen in a moment, in the twinkling of an eye, when the last trumpet is blown. For there will be a trumpet blast from the sky and all the Christians who have died will suddenly become alive, with new bodies that will never, never die; and then we who are still alive shall suddenly have new bodies too. For our earthly bodies, the ones we have now that can die, must be transformed into heavenly bodies that cannot perish but will live forever. When this happens, then at last this Scripture will come true—"Death is swallowed up in victory." O death, where then your victory? Where then your sting?[3]

For the Lord himself will come down from heaven with a mighty shout and with the soul-stirring cry of the archangel and the great trumpet-call of God. And the believers who are dead will be the first to rise to meet the Lord. Then we who are still alive and remain on the earth will be caught up with them in the clouds to meet the Lord in the air and remain with him forever. So comfort and encourage each other with this news.[4]

We are also told these wonderful but solemn facts:

Remember, each of us will stand personally before the Judgment Seat of God. For it is written, "As I live," says the Lord, "every knee shall bow to me and every tongue

2. 2 Thessalonians 1:7,8 TLB
3. 1 Corinthians 15:51–55 TLB
4. 1 Thessalonians 4:16–18 TLB

confess to God." Yes, each of us will give an account of himself to God.[5]

So our aim is to please him always in everything we do, whether we are here in this body or away from this body and with him in heaven. For we must all stand before Christ to be judged and have our lives laid bare—before him. Each of us will receive whatever he deserves for the good or bad things he has done in his earthly body. It is because of this solemn fear of the Lord, which is ever present in our minds, that we work so hard to win others. God knows our hearts, that they are pure in this matter, and I hope that, deep within, you really know it too.[6]

An Eternal Difference

Why do I stress this? Because it makes an eternal difference to you as to whether your life here on earth is lived according to Christ's directions. He directs you to love Him, to give Him your body, mind, and spirit, and to put God and others before yourself. You are to grow in understanding as you read God's Word and put it into practice in your life. You are to renounce evil, self-gratification, and selfishness of every kind.

Is the Christian life too hard? Yes, indeed it is, unless you let the Holy Spirit have control of your life. He gives strength to turn your mind from evil to good—but you must cooperate and use that strength available to you.

What is the result? At Christ's judgment of Christians He will tell you, "Well done, good and faithful servant; you were faithful over a few things, I will make you ruler over many things. Enter into the joy of your lord."[7]

Please note that although the Bible is full of instruc-

5. Romans 14:10–12 TLB
6. 2 Corinthians 5:9–11 TLB
7. Matthew 25:21 NKJV

tions warning us against displeasing God, and instructions telling us how to please Him, we *do* displease Him at times. Yet He has full forgiveness for us when we confess our sins to Him. *Even so, we must one day stand before God as His children and review our lives and receive His approval or disapproval, and His reward in accordance with how we have spent our lives as Christians.*

That our deeds here on earth are recorded in heaven is further stressed by Jesus when He told His disciples: "Don't store up treasures here on earth where they can erode away or may be stolen. Store them in heaven where they will never lose their value, and are safe from thieves. If your profits are in heaven your heart will be there too."[8]

8. Matthew 6:19–21 TLB

PART FOUR

Fulfilling God's Plan

Chapter Twelve

God has given each of us the ability to do certain things well.
Romans 12:6a TLB

Using Your God-Given Gifts for Him

God has a job for you! I'm not speaking now about your career (although He has arranged that for you, too), but about how to help your brother and sister Christians—and to help those who are still outside of God's special family.

Am I saying that you are to be a preacher or a missionary? No, not at all. There are many ways to do God's work, and He will help you do it well. Some people are called to work and live for God in factories, offices, classrooms, or farms. Whatever your daily work, you are to radiate Christ to those around you, as the fruitfulness of the Holy Spirit pours through your life to them.

And the Holy Spirit gives special abilities to each of us, to benefit His people. Here are some of them:[1]

- Offering wise advice
- Possessing supernatural knowledge

1. See 1 Corinthians 12:8–11; Romans 12

- Having special faith
- Healing the sick
- Doing miracles
- Prophesying
- Preaching
- Discerning evil spirits
- Having the gift of tongues (speaking in unknown languages)
- Interpreting the unknown languages
- Helping others
- Teaching God's Word
- Having money to give away
- Demonstrating administrative ability
- Comforting the sorrowing

There are many others. God gives you one or more divinely appointed abilities so that you can help your new brothers and sisters in the church. You are now a part of Christ's body, and His body has many parts, of which you are one. Each part, if it does its work well, is helping the whole body here on earth to function smoothly and well in accomplishing God's purposes. If you don't use the ability God gives you to help His church, the body will be weaker and less effective than it should be, and God will be saddened.

What Are Your Talents?

Has God given you one or more special talents? Think of your strengths and of how you can use them for Him.

If you find you have the ability to teach a Sunday school class without boring your students, then you have the gift of teaching—so use it!

If you can't identify your gift, consult Christian friends

and let them help you decide. Perhaps God has entrusted more than one of these gifts to you. Good! Whatever your gift or gifts, start by deciding how best to use your God-given talent for God, always depending on the Holy Spirit to empower you.

Remember, too, that you can ask God to give you talents and to help you develop them for His glory.[2] If your church needs a Sunday school teacher, perhaps God will give you a teaching gift. Don't be afraid to take some lessons or learn some child psychology as one of God's means of answering your prayer.

The Importance of Love

I know a woman and her husband who enjoy inviting people into their home and offering any encouragement or counsel they can, perhaps to a family with children, or a widow, or a student. They have a God-given gift of loving hospitality.

Pay close attention to this supreme fact: No matter how well you use your gift, it doesn't count for much in God's eyes unless it is used with love. A gift of helping others, or of giving money, if it is offered reluctantly, isn't what God wants at all. God only wants cheerful givers.

Your God-given ability can be used for your own gain rather than for the good of others. What a tragedy! If God gives you the ability to make money, it isn't so that you can buy better cars and furniture, but rather to give away:

> For God, who gives seed to the farmer to plant, and later on, good crops to harvest and eat, will give you more and

2. See 1 Corinthians 14:12

more seed to plant and will make it grow so that you can give away more and more fruit from your harvest.

Yes, God will give you much so that you can give away much, and when we take your gifts to those who need them they will break out into thanksgiving and praise to God for your help. So, two good things happen as a result of your gifts—those in need are helped, and they overflow with thanks to God. Those you help will be glad not only because of your generous gifts to themselves and to others, but they will praise God for this proof that your deeds are as good as your doctrine. And they will pray for you with deep fervor and feelings because of the wonderful grace of God shown through you.[3]

The same principle applies to each gift. Whatever talent you have—give it away. That is the purpose for which God gave it to you.

3. 2 Corinthians 9:10–14 TLB

Chapter Thirteen

Trust in the Lord with all your heart, and lean not on your own understanding; in all your ways acknowledge Him, and He shall direct your paths.

Proverbs 3:5,6 NKJV

Making Right Decisions

Finding a Spiritual Counselor

Remember, you are no longer alone. You are part of a family—the family of God. And all of us as God's children are to help one another. Your brothers and sisters are commanded to help you, and you are commanded to help them.

As a new Christian you need someone to be your spiritual counselor, to pray for you and with you. You need someone whose judgment you can trust to assist you in staying on God's pathway and to challenge and encourage you to be what you should be and to live as you should live.

A man should have a man for a counselor, and a woman should have a woman. Find someone who is willing to take the time to pray and counsel with you. Pray for such a relationship. Perhaps your spiritual counselor will be the one who led you to the Lord, or someone you became acquainted with in a small group in your church. Of course, you may turn to more than one person for help from time to time.

God, your ultimate Counselor, often speaks through the comments and advice of His people. As I have said, you are now part of the family of God, with many, many brothers and sisters. Some of them have a special gift from the Lord of spiritual wisdom and understanding. They can offer you sound advice or help you just by listening. When you need to think through a problem, consider the Christians you know—sometimes an older person with many experiences, but sometimes a gifted person of your own age or even younger.

Remember, too, that some who counsel may be separated from the will of God and may be wrong. Don't blindly follow any advice. When your own conscience is attuned to God—and be sure that it is—then you will be able to recognize and accept true counsel from others concerning important decisions. Take time to think about a matter; weigh it over carefully; pray about it.

Listen Carefully to Your Conscience

I remember so vividly and with such shame a time when I wanted to buy a business that I had no reason to buy! It was a good business and no moral issue was involved in the business itself, but it posed a big spiritual issue for me personally. The trouble was that I wanted to buy the business because I thought it would help to make me a bright star in the community and also make me rich. I knew my motives were wrong, but I tried to suppress them and silence my conscience and the voice of God telling me no. In football language there were "red flags" all over the field, but I insisted. After I bought the business, God in His grace made it go sour through a whole series of misfortunes. I finally sold it—in fact, I gave it away. Of course, I had a very great financial loss, but it was one of the best things that ever could have happened to me. It was God's discipline to tell me to behave myself next time—to listen to His voice and follow His will and not go wandering away on my own.

When you must make decisions, use all of the privileges God has given you. Learn to rely not only on Christian brothers and sisters to counsel with you, but also on the direct work of the Holy Spirit in your life. After prayer and submission to God, a deep internal feeling of yes or no often becomes a settled conviction.

The Apostle James tells us that when we require wisdom we only need to ask God for it. He will give it to us if we pray in faith, and if we ask for it to reflect God's glory and not our own.

Here again you can see how important Bible study is in teaching you the principles of right living. Your daily devotional Bible reading brings you into the very presence of God so that you stay fully yielded to Him and anxious to do His will in particular situations. God wants you to know His will, and He will gladly tell you what it is if you ask, listen, and are ready and willing to do what He says.

Evaluate Your Options

Sometimes in making a decision it helps to write out the reasons why or why not to follow a proposed course of action—list the pros and cons.

Take a sheet of paper and make a line down the middle so that you have two columns. In the right-hand column put the reasons why you *should not* do it and in the left-hand column the reasons why you *should* do it.

The actual number of reasons counts less than the qual-

ity and value and weight of each reason. Give a rating of
one to ten for each reason. Perhaps one reason merits a
heavy nine or ten while a half-dozen other reasons de-
serve only light ones. One high-ranking reason in the left-
hand column may outweigh several reasons in the other
column.

The Holy Spirit will help you to evaluate and value the
reasons if you are in a right relationship to Him. Let the
peace of God rule in your heart and mind—that is, in
your feelings and in your thinking.

A Caution

Be wary of dogmatic counselors who insist on dictato-
rial morality. Often, this kind of teaching springs from
factually inadequate personal opinion rather than from
biblical truth. Such counselors will be of little help to
you. Try someone else.

Stopped Short

I remember the time when my family was young and
growing and it seemed a natural thing to buy a house
rather than continue to rent. My wife and I prayed about
it for several days and felt no objection from the Lord, but
rather a feeling that we should investigate and explore the
possibilities. We found a half-finished house that was
within our buying range if I finished it up myself in my
spare time. My wife pointed out that I didn't *have* spare
time, and moreover I was not experienced or even tal-
ented as a builder. She obviously didn't think my plan
would work. But when we were unable to find anything
else within our price range, I decided to buy the house,
despite my wife's doubts about the wisdom of the pur-
chase. Much to my disappointment when I arrived to

close the deal, I was too late—someone else had already bought it. (Since then I have learned to trust my wife's judgment as much or more than my own, and if we don't agree on something, we don't do it.)

Soon afterward we found a house that was old but clean and sound. It had more room than the ''lost'' house had, and we could buy on contract with the money we had available. Both of us agreed this time, and we bought the house and lived in it for many happy years. The Lord answered prayer by blocking one way and bounding me into the right situation.

The opportunity to make right decisions is one of the many privileges God has given you. Ask Him, trust Him, make the decision, do His will, and learn as you go along.

Chapter Fourteen

But if we walk in the light as He is in the light, we have fellowship with one another.

1 John 1:7a NKJV

Joining a Local Church

Join God's Family

At the very moment that you became a Christian, you were adopted into the family of God. Now you have all of God's children as your family too. God loves you with the special love He has for those who love His Son. This family is to praise God together and to help one another, but this is impractical except on a local basis. You can love millions of people in God's family in only a very general way, yet you can help and be helped by your brothers and sisters in a local church.

That is why God has instructed us to join together in local fellowships. He says, "Let us not neglect our church meetings, as some people do."[1] At the time the Apostle Paul wrote these words, the same problem existed that we have today—some people weren't going to church. Paul says this neglect is dangerous.

It is dangerous because you are surrounded by people

---

1. Hebrews 10:25 TLB

whose goals are for the things of this life. Their goals are here on this earth, while yours are now in heaven. If you spend time only with people who are going their own ways and trying to figure out their own ways through life, you will find it difficult to stand against the tide. Your enthusiasm for Christ can soon become diluted or even obliterated.

That is why God tells us to meet together regularly with other Christians for praise and worship of God and for the study of His Word. If you neglect this discipline, you do it at your spiritual peril. A piece of kindling set on fire and laid by itself in a fireplace will soon go out; but if there are several pieces, the flame grows brighter and brighter and can set the whole world on fire!

Where Should I Look?

God commands fellowship, and you recognize its importance. Now the practical question is where to find a suitable fellowship.

Local churches come in all varieties. There are many different denominations: Baptist, Presbyterian, Assemblies of God, Methodist, and so on. In fact, I checked in an almanac once and discovered that there were more than a hundred denominations listed. They all have people in them who love the Lord and who are your brothers and sisters.

Why are there so many? Usually there is some historical difference of opinion on the interpretation of some verse of Scripture. Baptism is a good example. The Bible tells us to be baptized, but it doesn't tell us how to go about it. Some people think the whole body should be immersed (Baptists hold this view), and others believe that water should be sprinkled or poured on the head (Presbyterians follow this custom). Since many Baptists feel that true baptism has not occurred without full immersion, they have their own churches where this belief is agreed upon. It is good to have various denominations where the members agree and are comfortable with one another. Then they can spend their time praising the Lord and working together for Him.

If you are an average new Christian, I think it would be perfectly proper for you to join any denomination where the people love the Lord, regardless of their particular teaching on some of these points. Do, however, be aware that some churches have ministers who do not accept all that the Bible teaches. This statement may be hard for you to believe, but it is true. If you sit under their ministry, you will lose out on some of the important truths from God. Thus it would probably be best for you not to attend such a church.

Important Doctrines

Here are some of the historic doctrines indicated to us in the Bible itself that should be taught in every church:

1. That there is one eternal, all–powerful God in three persons: the Father, the Son, and the Holy Spirit.
2. That Jesus, God's Son, was born to a virgin.
3. That He lived a sinless life.
4. That He died for us, in our place, taking upon Himself God's wrath against our sins.
5. That He came back to life again.
6. That He ascended into heaven and is there with the Father, preparing our future home, while at the same time being personally present with each of us.

7. That the Holy Spirit, the third member of the Godhead, lives within us.
8. That Christ will return.
9. That Christians will face the judgment of Christ, not to find out whether their sins have been forgiven (for that was settled at the Cross when Jesus died for us), but for the deeds done during our lifetime on earth as Christians.
10. That Scripture is God's Word to us. The church where the Bible is not taught and where Christ is not the center is not a place for you as a new Christian.

Perhaps there are exceptional situations that indicate you should stay in a church where the Bible is not the authority. If you have been brought up in such a church, where these truths of the Bible are not taught, you might under some circumstances want to stay so that you can teach a Sunday school class, to serve and help other people. But, generally speaking, go to a church where *you* will be fed.

Beware of Cults

Another caution concerns the so-called cults. The cult is usually led by a very strong, charismatic leader who insists on rigid obedience to his or her every whim. There are Christians in some cults, but it is better to stay away from such groups.

Some cults believe only some of the Bible. They use certain verses (proof texts, as they are sometimes called) to support their doctrine. They may use a particular verse out of context, so that what is taught may be the opposite of what the Bible really says. This environment is not healthy for a new Christian.

The Electronic Church

What about staying home and watching church services on television, or listening to a minister on the radio? You will lose a lot if you limit yourself to these sources. One of God's means of grace is to direct us toward warm personal fellowship with others who name His name. Worshiping alone in your daily devotional time is extremely important; but so is worshiping in praise and prayer together, and listening to the Word of God as it is read and preached to a body of Christians.

Not an Option

So church attendance is *not* an option; it is a basic requirement. Remember too that church attendance is not only for your benefit but so that you can be helpful to others. Take the initiative if it is a "cold" church and warm it up with a happy smile and greeting. Perhaps some people have been members for so long, and became Christians so long ago, that they need to be reminded by your attitude to love the Lord with all their hearts, minds, and souls.

The pastor may not be the best preacher in the world, but people can become tired of even the best preaching unless they apply what is said to their lives with the help of the Holy Spirit. Even poor preaching can be used, or at least the worship service can be very valuable, if you look for the Lord's blessing in it.

If you seem to be constantly criticizing something in your church, then the first thing to do is to examine your own life and ask God to help you appreciate what is good rather than criticize what isn't. Then, if necessary, join another fellowship where you feel more at home. It won't be perfect, either, but it may better fit your needs at this particular time.

In any church, whether large or small, one can be lost in a crowd, and you need to learn to say a friendly hello to others who may be as reserved as you are. They need the contact with you just as you need the contact with your brothers and sisters in worship of the one Lord. To sing together before the Lord is important. Don't neglect it.

Begin to become involved in the activities of the church. The minimum, of course, is attendance; but you will want to contribute time and talent and money along with the others. You all need one another.

Outreach

The focus of your Christian outreach can be the immediate neighborhood through home Bible study groups or it can be your church or the entire community through a variety of volunteer activities.

Neighborhood

If you, as a representative of Christ, choose to bring His message to those in your neighborhood, a way to do this is through home Bible study classes for your neighbors.

Who will teach these classes? Perhaps you have a teaching talent. But not everyone reading this book has such a God-given ability and some don't who think they do! Get advice and counsel from others as to their opinion of your ability before attempting to teach a home Bible study. If you don't have a teaching gift but do have a home you can open in hospitality, perhaps you can find a teacher or use one of the scores of good group Bible study manuals that group members can take turns in leading. Stop by your local Christian bookstore, and use their catalogs to locate such materials.

Church and Community

Another way of service is to teach a Sunday school class, assist in the nursery, or participate in the youth groups in your church. Consider conducting services in your local jail. Get in touch with the chaplain if there is one; and if there is not, talk to the person in charge of the jail and ask permission to talk to the prisoners. Bringing a bit of comfort and cheer to someone in a nursing home or retirement center can reap rich rewards in heaven, and sometimes deep satisfaction here on earth.

Spiritual Reinforcement

Is church attendance important? The answer is a resounding yes! Can you worship God by observing the beauties of nature, by walking in the woods, or by jogging? Sure, you can worship God and pray anywhere, but private devotion is not God's full plan for you.

Meeting together with other brothers and sisters as a church family is required for maximum development of the spiritual life. Read the first chapters of the book of Acts and notice how often reference is made to the new Christians meeting together for prayer and worship. Remember the Apostle Paul's warning: "Let us not neglect our church meetings, as some people do, but encourage and warn each other, especially now that the day of his coming back again is drawing near."[2]

Why is such fellowship important?

2. Hebrews 10:25 TLB

Remember the kindling stick! When it is lit and laid on the ground or in a fireplace by itself, it tends to go out soon. If it is added to other kindling sticks, the heat is reinforced, and soon there is a blazing fire. So it is spiritually. Each of us cannot stand alone easily. The church is one of the great means God has given us to help us become all that He wants us to be. We neglect this, His will, at our spiritual peril.

Chapter Fifteen

It is possible to give away and become richer! It is also possible to hold on too tightly and lose everything.

Proverbs 11:24 TLB

Giving to God

Have you ever heard the word *tithing?* Tithing means to give back one-tenth of your income to God. Moses gave this law to the Israelites three thousand years ago. They gave one-tenth of their crops to the priests of God. In today's world we give to God by contributing to the church, or to the poor through various charities, or to missionaries so that they can tell others about God.

More than Tithing

But God requires more than tithing from us. His requirement for us today is higher! We are to give back all of our selves and our income to God, and then let Him tell us how much is to be used for ourselves and our families, and how much should be given to Him for His work. The Apostle Paul discusses this issue:

> But remember this—if you give little, you will get little. A farmer who plants just a few seeds will get only a small crop, but if he plants much, he will reap much. Every one must make up his own mind as to how much he should give. Don't force anyone to give more than he really wants to, for

cheerful givers are the ones God prizes. God is able to make it up to you by giving you everything you need and more, so that there will not only be enough for your own needs, but plenty left over to give joyfully to others. It is as the Scriptures say: "The godly man gives generously to the poor. His good deeds will be an honor to him forever." For God, who gives seed to the farmer to plant, and later on, good crops to harvest and eat, will give you more and more seed to plant and will make it grow so that you can give away more and more fruit from your harvest. Yes, God will give you much so that you can give away much.[1]

Note several facts that are presented in these verses:

1. God is interested in cheerful givers. If you give under a sense of reluctant obligation, there is no point in giving.
2. God gives to you so that you can give to others, blessing them and yourself at the same time.
3. Your gift will be an honor to you forever.
4. When you give, God gives you opportunities for more income so you can give away more.
5. Christ lays it on the line: "For neither you nor anyone else can serve two masters. You will hate one and show loyalty to the other, or else the other way around—you will be enthusiastic about one and despise the other. You cannot serve both God and money."[2]
6. This is a basic, spiritual decision you must make. Give God that key too, or live a life of frustration.

Here is a practical question for you to consider: Should

---

1. 2 Corinthians 9:6–11 TLB
2. Luke 16:13 TLB

I give to God when I can barely support myself or my family? What does God want me to do? The answer of many who have faced this situation is that God honors the faith of the giver and takes care of the family's needs too. Try it and see.

Doubtless there are people in your church who are in special need. Why not help them, perhaps with an anonymous gift? Then consider the Salvation Army and other excellent channels for giving to those outside your church, for whom you feel God's love and responsibility. Hundreds of statements in the Scriptures tell us that we should help the poor, for example, "If anyone so much as gives you a cup of water because you are Christ's—I say this solemnly—he won't lose his reward."[3]

Certainly part of your income should go overseas to reach people there with the saving message of Christ's love. Famine relief, Bible translation work, missionary salaries, assistance to national pastors overseas—all these are fully worthy of your prayers and gifts.

"You can't outgive God" is a true statement. Give to Him by giving to the poor and to His church, and He will return it to you "pressed down,...and running over."[4] "For others will treat you as you treat them."[5] "Cast your bread upon the waters, for you will find it after many days."[6]

---

3. Mark 9:41 TLB
4. Luke 6:38 TLB
5. Matthew 7:2 TLB
6. Ecclesiastes 11:1 NKJV

Tithing Your Time

Time is one of the greatest assets God has given you. When you were born, you were given a bag of gold coins, one for each day of your life. These coins are time, and they disappear one by one, day by day, from the day of your birth.

How will you use your coins? For eternity, I hope. God wants each of us to use part of each day's time for work, for play, for study, for family, for friends, for Him. In the past you haven't given much thought to using your time for God. It's easy to spend time (or sometimes waste it) on the affairs of this earth. Suddenly your priorities are all changed because you have placed yourself firmly into the ways of God.

Just as your money all belongs to God, so does your time. How does He want you to use it? If you take 10 per cent—a tithe of your day—that means 10 per cent of the fifteen hours you are awake each day; that is, one-and-a-half hours for God. Prayer, Bible reading, and study time are an important part of your time tithe. What are some other ways to give God your time? Here are a few:

- Visit patients in the hospital.
- Participate in a prison ministry.
- Invite friends and acquaintances for a meal at your home, where God will be honored.
- Offer your time to the church, whether to lead or to help paint, count the offering, be an usher, teach a Sunday school class, or change diapers in the nursery. Do whatever your talents lead you to do.
- Read books that will broaden your understanding of God and His world.

- Help widows or elderly singles who need lawns cut, or take them to church meetings, or just be their friend. If you are a college student, perhaps someone down the hall is in need of a friend; a friendly act will make his or her day. Use your God-given imagination to its fullest.
- Consider teaching or inviting neighbors and friends to a home Bible study or being a host or hostess for these occasions.

Sit down now with a pencil and paper (or use the margin of this page) and think and pray about various ways to spend God's time. Then decide when to begin, perhaps today. (If the TV or radio is on, turn it off while you are doing this!)

Giving to God out of your resources of money, time, and talent is at once an obligation and an opportunity. It is a wonderfully strange paradox that the more we give, the more we receive. The more we give of ourselves to Christ, the more spiritually rich we become.

Chapter Sixteen

From a wise mind comes careful and persuasive speech.
Proverbs 16:23 TLB

Sharing Jesus with Others

A Prayer Challenge

We are told by our Lord to go into all the world (including next door) and preach the good news. But not all of us will do it the same way. Some people can easily get into a conversation that leads to discussion of the Bible and its message. If you are like many others who find it difficult or are uncomfortable or afraid to tell others about what Christ has done for you and for them, here is a prayer challenge for you. Ask the Lord Jesus and His Holy Spirit to give you strength and joy and excitement in sharing.

People you work with or go to school with should know you are a Christian. This fact should be evident to them because of your kindness and good deeds, because you are not participating in all the wrong things going on around you, and because of your comments and remarks. As you have the opportunity, tell them what the Lord Jesus means to you in your life. Talk about answers to prayer you have received. People are almost always interested, even fascinated, when hearing such reports.

The Importance of Actions

May it never be said that your friends don't know you are a Christian. But on the other hand, may it never be said that you talk like a Christian but don't act like one! How terrible that would be, and what an insult to our God who sent His Son to give you an entirely new kind of life.

Methods

Some Christians keep Bible excerpts or other booklets on hand to give to interested people. Certainly it is a valuable way of sharing Christ with others. Perhaps it is even better to have a modern language version of the New Testament or Bible to loan out to others. Ask God to help you find someone who has never read the Bible very much (probably thinking it is unreadable), but who would like to give it a try. Then the Holy Spirit can use God's Word to strike deeply into this person's heart and mind. By loaning, instead of giving, there is more likelihood that it will be read, and you will have the opportunity to discuss what is being read under your supervision.

Some people are natural born extroverts and can easily explain to others why they feel as they do about God and our Lord Jesus. Others couldn't sell coal to Eskimos and wouldn't want to try! Temperament and personality make a lot of difference as to how we tell others about our faith, but all of us are responsible to let others know where we stand. Even the most timid people here in America can identify themselves as Christians without embarrassment. A generation ago this would have caused at least some eyebrow lifting, and perhaps a laugh of derision. Today it is easier. People have interest and concern about religion. Christ's people are not permitted by their Lord to withdraw into their shells and be secret believers.

Millions of people in America are looking for something better spiritually than they have now. Their lives are frustrated, unhappy, discouraged, and broken, even though they may be smiling outwardly. You have in your possession joy, peace, and all the other good things given by the Holy Spirit to those who trust in Him. How can your wonderful message of deliverance be imparted to the hungry, despairing hearts of others? The very first step is to let them know that you yourself have peace and that it is available to them too. There are other ways for you to tell the good news to others, and I will mention some of them here.

At some appropriate time ask whether he or she would be interested in having you explain what a Christian really is. Then use ''The Four Spiritual Laws'' or some other simple system of explanation.

The Four Spiritual Laws

1. God *loves* you, and offers a wonderful *plan* for your life.

2. Man is *sinful* and *separated* from God. Therefore, he cannot know and experience God's love and plan for his life.

3. Jesus Christ is God's *only* provision for man's sin. Through Him you can know and experience God's love and plan for your life.

4. We must individually *receive* Jesus Christ as Savior and Lord; then we can know and experience God's love and plan for our lives.[1]

1. For the complete Four Spiritual Laws, see the appendix on page 173.

You can receive Christ right now through prayer.

Other Ideas

Loan Christian books. Just as with Bibles, it's often better to loan books rather than to give them. The reason is not economic, but psychological—a person is more likely to read what you loan to him if he must return it to you, with an implied obligation to comment upon what he has read.

Become enthusiastic about being a Christian! Spend enough regular time with God in Bible reading and prayer to realize how "lucky" you are to know and experience His love. Then you will be eager to share these good things with others.

Be friendly and helpful to all people—not as a bait you will discontinue if you don't succeed in winning them, but constantly as part of your Christian life-style and inner attitude.

Invite them to come along with you to church or to some special Christian meetings.

Invite them to your home for a meal.

Invite the neighbors in for a film or video presentation, with a discussion afterward.[2]

Invite them to a Bible study.

Remember, too, that you are a link in a chain. You sow the good seed, others water it, and eventually the harvest comes. You don't have to do it all—the sowing, watering,

---

2. Tim Timmons and Stephen Arterburn's *Hooked on Life* (Nashville: Oliver-Nelson and Nelson Communications, 1985) is excellent for this purpose. Ask your local Christian bookstore for information on books, audio and video resources, film rental, related printed material, and action groups.

and reaping, too—though God may give you this entire privilege.

Don't ever forget about the need to nurture newborn Christians. Don't leave them to fend for themselves. Help them get started in Bible study, a prayer life, a church fellowship, a new life-style, if needed, and in sharing their new faith with others. Becoming a Christian starts with an overwhelmingly important *decision,* but it must be followed by a lifelong *process.*

PART FIVE

Facing Some Issues

Chapter Seventeen

We can always "prove" that we are right, but is the Lord convinced?

Proverbs 16:2 TLB

Questions and Answers

I have tried to answer here some of the questions often asked by new Christians. Because you are a young Christian, the entire landscape is so new that you may have questions about things I don't see because I've looked at them too often. So don't forget all that I've said earlier in this book about getting help from your new brothers and sisters, from your pastor or personal counselor, and from the Holy Spirit through the Word of God, the Bible.

Meanwhile, here we go:

What is "speaking in tongues"?

"Speaking in tongues" is an expression used in the Bible. It means for someone to be empowered by the Holy Spirit to speak in a language he or she has never learned and doesn't understand. These may be languages spoken somewhere in the world but unknown to the speaker, or languages not of this world but known only to angels and the Holy Spirit.

This phenomenon is told about in the Bible.[1] Just before Christ rose into the clouds and departed for heaven, He told His disciples to wait in Jerusalem until the Holy Spirit came upon them and that He (the Holy Spirit) would remain with them forever. A few days later, as the disciples met together, suddenly a loud sound like a rushing, mighty wind from heaven filled the entire house where they were gathered. Then they saw what seemed to be tongues of fire resting on each of them. They all were filled with the Holy Spirit, and they began to speak in languages they didn't know, for the Spirit gave them this ability.

Should all Christians "speak in tongues"?

The Apostle Paul tells us that this is only one of many different gifts which God gives to His people, and not all have the same gift.[2] Those who have this gift may use it in church meetings, but only if someone is present who has the God-given ability to understand what the speaker in tongues is saying.

Many excellent Bible scholars believe that the gift of speaking in tongues began and ended with the apostles, while other excellent Bible scholars disagree and believe the gift continues today. You will need to study the matter for yourself and come to your own conclusion. Even if you are not sure that the gift of tongues is for today, you may want to become a member of a church that believes it does continue, because of the warmth and joy expressed in many of these churches. In any event, the Apostle Paul

1. See Acts 2
2. See 1 Corinthians 12:4–31 and 1 Corinthians 14:1–33,39,40

is very clear in his statement, "never forbid speaking in tongues."[3] But the rules he lays down must be followed.

What about evolution?

Evolutionists believe that man evolved from protoplasm formed by natural elements that happened to meet in right proportions in some prehistoric sea, perhaps aided by a propitious bolt of lightning at that exact moment and place, to congeal the elements into life. Or, they say, no one knows how the first amoebalike substance began, but obviously it did, and eventually it evolved into man, for here we are.

This explanation begs too many questions to count. All one can say is, "Yes, perhaps it could have happened that way." But let no sensible person say, "Yes, that is the way it happened!" Many top scientists are now saying that evolution is far from a proven fact. One of the big problems lies in explaining how complex organs—the eye, for instance, or the sex organs—gradually developed when there was no use for them until they were fully formed. To solve this, the latest theory is macroevolution—the belief that one day from an eyeless worm (or whatever) an offspring was born with all the needed nerve ganglia and eye structures. Even more surprising, male and female offspring suddenly came from an asexual organism, at the same time and place, so that they would have the opportunity to mate.

The genetic structure of the human cell is another incredible surprise to an objective observer. The DNA code

---

3. 1 Corinthians 14:39 TLB

apparatus in every cell is, to say the least, amazing. How did it "develop"?

Again, the usual answer of academia is, "We don't know. But since creation by God is impossible, evolution is the best we can think of."

Well, who says creation by God is impossible? That statement is considered a scientific "given," and those challenging it are thought absurd. But, of course, there is at least equal if not far greater absurdity in the usual "scientific" explanation.

So what does the Christian do? Lose his or her faith because "science" says the Bible is all wet when it declares that God created the earth and man?[4] That is certainly quite unnecessary!

Another important point to remember is that the Bible doesn't give dates for man's appearance. The Hebrew word *yom,* translated "day" in the Genesis creation account, elsewhere in the Bible is used to mean other than twenty-four hours. Another equally valid translation of *yom* is "age." That is why many Bible scholars believe that instead of all creation occurring in six twenty-four-hour days, it took place during six ages, each millions of years in length. God created life in stages, they think, with man and woman being created after the various ages of plants, fish, birds, and animals. How long ago? Geological and archaeological evidence may indicate that man has been around for millions of years. But some expert Christian scientists opt for thousands of years rather than millions. No one really knows.

Is it reasonable to think that God created man from the

4. See Genesis 1 and 2 TLB

dust of the earth, as the Bible declares? A minor miracle, really, in comparison with the exploding of a fingerful of mass into billions of stars traveling away from us at the rate of millions of miles an hour into limitless space. Where did the space come from? When and where did time begin? Do space and time ever begin or end? Apparently not!

Is it important to buy and read Christian books?

Yes, because doing this can accelerate your understanding of the Bible and its application to your life. A few minutes or more of Bible instruction each week from a sermon at church isn't nearly enough. Your daily Bible reading adds wonderfully; but you need to see all aspects of the Bible on important themes. Through a book you can profit from the careful Bible study of someone who has spent years researching and writing. You receive the fruit of his or her labor for the price of an hour of your earnings. But books are too expensive? Yes, they cost the price of a hamburger or two. If you really don't have the money to buy Christian books, ask God for it. (Or visit your church's library, if it has one.)

Are family devotions important?

Yes. The time spent as a family reading the Bible and praying gives children (and parents too) a tremendous start in Christian understanding. Innumerable thousands of children realize Christ as Savior and Lord as a result of these family times together. Let it be a time—in fact, *make* it a time—for applying the Bible to daily life at school, business, and play.

This family time also should be used for reading

books—secular as well as Christian. Try Mother Goose and similar children's classics; as the children grow older, try C. S. Lewis's Narnia series, *Pilgrim's Progress, Swiss Family Robinson,* and *Mutiny on the Bounty.* Use this opportunity, at least from kindergarten on, to discuss good things (as well as bad) that happen at school, and entertain questions by each member of the family. Let it be a time of openness and explanation, not a time of being scolded or disciplined.

How much time should be allowed for television, video cassettes or video games?

As little as possible. There are special series you should watch as a family; and for relaxation try some good nature shows and current event discussions on the public network. But the person spending more than a half-hour or so a day on regular network programs is probably using precious time unwisely. The average person spends several hours a day in front of the tube. What is happening to them and to their families? There are two problems relating to this.

The first is that in many cases there is a reduction of family communication, with family members sitting silent before the TV set, rather than interacting profitably with each other in conversation.

The second problem is that some people—especially some men—are drawn toward dirty jokes, innuendoes, and more and more explicitness in sexual matters, and the media masters are happy to supply this demand. So most television programs are becoming more and more attuned to base desires. The Christian viewer, though at first objecting, gradually accepts what is clearly evil and against the command of God. Thus God's child gets hooked on Satan's depraved plans and programs.

I was around when television was just getting started, and I remember so vividly visiting a wealthy Christian family that had had a set for several months. I was more than surprised when a humorous skit was shown of "The Lady and the Ape." In this episode the ape was making sexual advances to the lady by trying to take off her jacket. While I watched in horror, these deeply spiritual—and I am not being sarcastic, they were—friends laughed uproariously at the lady's antics in foiling the ape. Bestiality is punishable by death under the Old Testament code, but this violation of God's law was being laughed at by God's people. They didn't realize how much they had become a part of the world in its disdain of God's laws and purposes.

Murder, rape, seduction, and profanity—all these are now common fare coming into the Christian home. I hope it is clear to you that exposure to these evils allows the enemy to live in your home and spend hour after hour in your inmost life, where the Holy Spirit is supposed to have complete sway.

Does this mean giving up television entirely? Quite possibly so, depending on whether you are able to control your television viewing habits. News reports, though very time consuming, are probably valid, as are occasional sports events if you are a sports fan (but "television widows" are certainly not God's plan for His people).

Are children's programs okay? Well, what are they teaching? Just this week a neighbor told me that her three-year-old daughter had begun lying. On interrogation, and after discussion and then a spanking when it continued, the little one tearfully exclaimed, "But the

135

Muppets do it all the time." (The Muppets are, as this is being written, a very popular children's puppet TV series.) Sure enough, when the parents watched the next day, the Muppets were lying to their teacher and it was all seen as very amusing and good fun. That is how the three-year-old learned that lying is okay. (No more Muppets in that family!)

And so it is that the media directors—the largest proportion of them being atheistic, nonchurchgoing humanists with no objection, for instance, to homosexuality and premarital sex (I'm quoting from a recent poll by a respected polling agency)—determine the spiritual and moral standards of TV for your family. Is this something you can allow in your Christian home? Or your own life? Will you let Satan's influences permeate your life and the lives of your children?

As to movies, you will need to use your own judgment. I personally attend infrequently. When I do, I am disgusted with the profanity and suggestive situations, especially the previews offering glimpses of bedroom scenes, rape, murder, and other ungodliness.

What Bible version should I use?

All versions are good, so use the one you can read and enjoy the most. The King James Version is the Bible on which most people in the forty-year-old-and-above age group were brought up—though many haven't read it very much. A number of people have now switched to versions easier to read without the *thees* and *thous* and obsolete words used 375 years ago.

If your pastor prefers the King James, or another version, but you prefer a different one, there is no point in

arguing. Spend a few extra dollars and use two transla-
tions—the one you enjoy and profit from in private reading, and the one to take to church for public reading and
study groups. There is no "best" translation. Use any
and all of them.

*I've been planning to be (or am now) a carpenter (or doctor
or whatever). Now that I am a Christian, should I go to
Bible school or seminary in order to become a pastor?*

No, probably not. The Apostle Paul says to new Christians: "So, dear brothers, whatever situation a person is
in when he becomes a Christian, let him stay there, for
now the Lord is there to help him."[5]

In other words, continue your present work or plans
until God shows you otherwise. Pray for a knowledge of
His will for your life. Don't act hastily. If He tells you to
stay where you are, use the opportunities for God where
you are and keep close to Him so you won't get side-
tracked into materialism and selfishness and love of
money. If God tells you to change your plans or to become a pastor, use exactly the same cautions, for Satan is
as actively employed to distract pastors as anyone else
from God's way.

How can I know God's will for my life?

It takes a bit of experience and practice. The first step is
to check again to see if you are willing to do God's will,
whatever it is and whatever the cost. Why should He
bother to tell you what He wants if you aren't going to
do it?

5. 1 Corinthians 7:24 TLB

The next step is to review in your mind the questions the Scriptures ask. Are your motives pure and clear—or are you seeking something for yourself—fame, fortune, popularity, or whatever? Or is your primary motive to help others?

With a pure conscience, pray for God's wisdom. He has promised it: "If you want to know what God wants you to do, ask him, and he will gladly tell you, for he is always ready to give a bountiful supply of wisdom to all who ask him; he will not resent it."[6]

If you are struggling to find God's will in a situation, you might try this method. Take a blank sheet of paper, draw a line down the center, and write the reasons *for* on one side of the line, and reasons *against* on the other side. Give a value ranging from a high of one to a low of ten to each reason:

What shall I do about:_____
(Write your question)

	YES	*Value*		NO	*Value*
1.	_____	____	*1.*	_____	____
2.	_____	____	*2.*	_____	____
3.	_____	____	*3.*	_____	____
4.	_____	____	*4.*	_____	____
5.	_____	____	*5.*	_____	____
6.	_____	____	*6.*	_____	____
7.	_____	____	*7.*	_____	____
	Total Value	____		*Total Value*	____

6. James 1:5 TLB

A few negatives with a high rating may outweigh many positives with low ratings; then the answer will be no. Or it may work the other way around.

The system isn't foolproof, but we are to use our God-directed minds to find God's will, and this is one way to approach it. Reasons listed for or against may well include your abilities, as well as your opportunities.

Consult an open-minded Christian friend. Go over your reasons pro and con and let him or her comment from Scripture and experience.

For many Christians—after thought, prayer and discussion—a settled conviction is God's answer. "And let the peace of God rule in your hearts, to which also you were called in one body; and be thankful."[7]

Should Christians use horoscopes?

In the Bible there are many prohibitions against witchcraft, divination and mediums.

> You must not...use fortune telling or witchcraft.[8]

> Do not defile yourselves by consulting mediums and wizards.[9]

> No Israeli may practice black magic, or call on the evil spirits for aid, or be a fortune teller,...or call forth the spirits of the dead.[10]

The same prohibitions apply to Ouija boards, seances, and palm readers. They are fakes controlled by evil spirits. Stay away!

---

7. Colossians 3:15 NKJV
8. Leviticus 19:26 TLB
9. Leviticus 19:31 TLB
10. Deuteronomy 18:10a,11 TLB

Sometimes I read or hear about modernists, liberals, fundamentalists, conservatives, evangelicals, charismatics, and the Moral Majority. What do these terms mean?

Let's take them one at a time:

Modernists and Liberals

These terms are equivalent. A hundred or so years ago the Bible was declared dead in most European and some American theological schools. Various scholars decided the Bible was a compilation of myths and should not be studied seriously. People agreeing with this description of the Bible were (and are) known as *modernists* (they take a "modern" view of the Bible instead of the church's traditional view) or *liberals* (they are "liberal" because of their acceptance of other religions and of nontraditional viewpoints about the Bible). The result of modernism and liberalism is the belief that Christ's death on the cross for our sins is not the way of salvation, or is not the only way. A further implication for some is to disbelieve in the God of the Bible, and to believe instead that there is no God (atheism) or that He is unknowable (agnosticism).

Fundamentalists

In the year 1918 a series of books called *The Fundamentals* was published concerning the truth of the Bible and its teachings. These books reaffirmed the doctrines held from the beginnings of the church by Christ and His apostles. These doctrines include the birth of Christ to a virgin, Mary; the truth and authority of the Bible; the death of Christ for our sins; His coming back to life again; the assurance that He will return again; and many other basic beliefs of the church. Most churches had quietly believed these things all along, but the publication of these books became a rallying cry for those who opposed the modernism and liberalism rapidly spreading in the theological schools and in some well-known churches.

Fundamentalism can be described as a return to purity of doctrine and to the authority of the Bible. However, some fundamentalists were caustic and unloving in their statements about liberals and modernists, with the result that many who agreed with the fundamentals of the Bible did not want to be known as harsh fundamentalists. What did they want to be called? Gradually they became known as conservatives.

Conservatives and Evangelicals

Conservatives and *Evangelicals* are people who believe the truths of the Bible but tend to preach Christ rather than spend time accusing those who deny the faith. They are a majority in most churches and are 100 per cent of the membership in many so-called Bible churches, which are independent of any denomination. Many denominations require all members to believe the historic creeds of Christ's church.

Charismatics (or Pentecostals)

Charismatics are conservatives who believe that the gift of tongues (speaking by the power of the Holy Spirit in unknown languages) is still given today and may be used in church meetings, usually in prayer. This movement began when several Pentecostal denominations sprang up in the early 1900s. In more recent years many non-denominational charismatic churches have begun. As a generalization, the denominational churches call themselves Pentecostals and believe that those who have never spoken in tongues have not received the fullness of the

Holy Spirit. Nondenominational churches which call themselves charismatics believe that the Holy Spirit gives the gift of tongues to some, but different gifts to others; and all can be equally filled with the Holy Spirit whether or not they have the gift of tongues.

The Moral Majority

This group is not a church. It includes people of many diverse religious and nonreligious persuasions who agree that America should return to the Bible's standards of morality.

What are cults?

These are religions that have some elements of Christianity but do not depend on the death and resurrection of Christ as the only way to God and to His forgiveness and blessings.

Are Mormons Christians? They have a strong family orientation and their young missionaries seem to be fine, upstanding people.

No one knows whether a particular person has received the Lord Jesus Christ as Savior and Lord. The Mormons as a church are not considered to be a Christian denomination, even though they have a high respect for Jesus and the Bible. The question to be asked is whether a Mormon or anyone else believes that the only way to God is through Jesus Christ, not through church membership, good deeds, secret rituals, or baptism for the dead.

What about the so-called Moonies? Are they Christians?

Do they consider Jesus, God's Son, as their only Messiah and only way to God? If not, they are not Christians.

Is Transcendental Meditation ("TM") Christian?

Meditation on the Bible is needed for Christian growth, but meditation, in the sense of emptying one's mind to let the winds blow in, can be dangerous. Our minds are to be filled with Christ and not open to His enemy. Repetition of a word or sound is not the Bible's way to Christian growth.

Can a guru help me?

No, our Master is the Lord Jesus Christ, and it is very dangerous to look elsewhere for guidance or control.

Isn't Christianity narrow-minded in excluding all other cults and religions?

Yes, that is certainly true. Christ claimed to be the only way to God, and proved it by His resurrection. He said, "I am the door. If anyone enters by Me, he will be saved...and find pasture. The thief does not come except to steal, and to kill, and to destroy. I have come that they may have life, and may have it more abundantly."[11]

11. John 10:9,10 NKJV

Chapter Eighteen

Guard my words as your most precious possession. Write them
down, and also keep them deep within your heart. Love wisdom like a sweetheart.

Proverbs 7:2b–4a TLB

Know the Bible

Memorizing Bible verses is very important. Just as with
information in a computer, if it isn't put in, it can't come
out and be applied to the problem at hand. True, you
may have a general or vague idea of what the Bible has to
say about a question you are facing, but having the appropriate summary verse rush to your aid is invaluable.

Moreover, the Bible is a means of helping others find
Christ, but they don't need to take your word for what it
says. Quote the Bible to them. It will often touch them
with special power as the Holy Spirit uses His own words
to reveal His truth to them.

But before you begin to memorize Bible verses, I suggest that you memorize the names and locations of the
books of the Bible. If you are in a Bible study group and
want to read a verse under discussion it takes too long to
look in the index of your Bible for the page number. Be
able to turn at once to the location because you know
where it is. Here are the Bible books in sequence, in
memory groups. Please memorize them.

Old Testament (39 Books)

Genesis	Job
Exodus	Psalms
Leviticus	Proverbs
Numbers	Ecclesiastes
Deuteronomy	Song of Solomon
Joshua	Isaiah
Judges	Jeremiah
Ruth	Lamentations
	Ezekiel
1 Samuel	Daniel
2 Samuel	
1 Kings	Hosea
2 Kings	Joel
1 Chronicles	Amos
2 Chronicles	Obadiah
Ezra	Jonah
Nehemiah	Micah
Esther	Nahum
	Habakkuk
	Zephaniah
	Haggai
	Zechariah
	Malachi

New Testament (27 Books)

Matthew	1 Thessalonians
Mark	2 Thessalonians
Luke	1 Timothy
John	2 Timothy
	Titus
Acts	
Romans	Philemon
1 Corinthians	Hebrews
2 Corinthians	James
Galatians	1 Peter
Ephesians	2 Peter
Philippians	1 John
Colossians	2 John
	3 John
	Jude
	Revelation

Now here are fifty-two verses for you to learn, one each week for a year. And don't forget to keep reviewing. Fix them in your mind for blessings each day here on earth and for eternity. The verses are designed to be cut out so that you may carry them with you.

Salvation

- -

"For God loved the world so much that he gave his only Son so that anyone who believes in him shall not perish but have eternal life."

John 3:16 TLB

- -

For by grace you have been saved through faith, and that not of yourselves; it is the gift of God, not of works, lest anyone should boast.

Ephesians 2:8,9 NKJV

- -

There is therefore now no condemnation to those who are in Christ Jesus, who do not walk according to the flesh, but according to the Spirit.

Romans 8:1 NKJV

- -

Not by works of righteousness which we have done, but according to His mercy He saved us, through the washing regeneration and renewing of the Holy Spirit.

Titus 3:5 NKJV

- -

"Most assuredly, I say to you, he who hears My word and believes in Him who sent Me has everlasting life, and shall not come into judgment, but has passed from death into life."

John 5:24 NKJV

Forgiveness

- -

In Him we have redemption through His blood, the forgiveness of sins, according to the riches of His grace.

Ephesians 1:7 NKJV

- -

If we confess our sins, He is faithful and just to forgive us our sins and to cleanse us from all unrighteousness.

1 John 1:9 NKJV

- -

"And you shall know the truth, and the truth shall make you free."

John 8:32 NKJV

- -

Bless the Lord, O my soul, and forget not all His benefits: Who forgives all your iniquities, Who heals all your diseases.

Psalm 103:2,3 NKJV

- -

"For if you forgive men their trespasses, your heavenly Father will also forgive you."

Matthew 6:14 NKJV

Faith

- -

Therefore, having been justified by faith, we have peace with God through our Lord Jesus Christ.

Romans 5:1 NKJV

- -

So then faith comes by hearing, and hearing by the word of God.

Romans 10:17 NKJV

- -

And be found in Him, not having my own righteousness, which is from the law, but that which is through faith in Christ, the righteousness which is from God by faith.

Philippians 3:9 NKJV

- -

But without faith it is impossible to please Him, for he who comes to God must believe that He is, and that He is a rewarder of those who diligently seek Him.

Hebrews 11:6 NKJV

- -

For whatever is born of God overcomes the world. And this is the victory that has overcome the world—our faith.

1 John 5:4 NKJV

Discipleship

- -

"But seek first the kingdom of God and His righteousness, and all these things shall be added to you."

Matthew 6:33 NKJV

- -

"Go therefore and make disciples of all the nations,
baptizing them in the name of the Father and of the Son
and of the Holy Spirit, teaching them to observe all
things that I have commanded you; and lo, I am with
you always, even to the end of the age."

Matthew 28:19,20 NKJV

- -

I beseech you therefore, brethren, by the mercies of
God, that you present your bodies a living sacrifice, holy,
acceptable to God, which is your reasonable service.

Romans 12:1 NKJV

- -

We then who are strong ought to bear with the scruples
of the weak, and not to please ourselves.

Romans 15:1 NKJV

- -

"By this all will know that you are My disciples, if you
have love for one another."

John 13:35 NKJV

"Assuredly, I say to you, inasmuch as you did it to one of the least of these My brethren, you did it to Me."

Matthew 25:40 NKJV

- -

Therefore, my beloved brethren, be steadfast, immovable, always abounding in the work of the Lord, knowing that your labor is not in vain in the Lord.

1 Corinthians 15:58 NKJV

- -

Do not love the world or the things in the world. If anyone loves the world, the love of the Father is not in him.

1 John 2:15 NKJV

God's Word

- -

All Scripture is given by inspiration of God, and is profitable for doctrine, for reproof, for correction, for instruction in righteousness, that the man of God may be complete, thoroughly equipped for every good work.

2 Timothy 3:16,17 NKJV

- -

Your word I have hidden in my heart, that I might not sin against You.

Psalm 119:11 NKJV

- -

This Book of the Law shall not depart from your mouth, but you shall meditate in it day and night, that you may observe to do according to all that is written in it. For then you will make your way prosperous, and then you will have good success.

Joshua 1:8 NKJV

- -

It is written, "Man shall not live by bread alone, but by every word that proceeds from the mouth of God."

Matthew 4:4 NKJV

- -

"The words that I speak to you are spirit, and they are life."

John 6:63b NKJV

Holding fast the word of life, so that I may rejoice in the day of Christ that I have not run in vain or labored in vain.

Philippians 2:16 NKJV

- -

For the word of God is living and powerful, and sharper than any two-edged sword, piercing even to the division of soul and spirit, and of joints and marrow, and is a discerner of the thoughts and intents of the heart.

Hebrews 4:12 NKJV

- -

And take the helmet of salvation and the sword of the spirit, which is the word of God.

Ephesians 6:17 NKJV

Witnessing

- -

"But you shall receive power when the Holy Spirit has come upon you; and you shall be witnesses to Me in Jerusalem, and in all Judea and Samaria, and to the end of the earth."

Acts 1:8 NKJV

- -

Come and hear, all you who fear God, and I will declare what He has done for my soul.

Psalm 66:16 NKJV

- -

Now we exhort you, brethren, warn those who are unruly, comfort the fainthearted, uphold the weak, be patient with all.

1 Thessalonians 5:14 NKJV

- -

But sanctify the Lord God in your hearts, and always be ready to give a defense to everyone who asks you a reason for the hope that is in you, with meekness and fear.

1 Peter 3:15 NKJV

Spiritual Resources

- -

"I am the vine, you are the branches. He who abides in Me, and I in him, bears much fruit; for without Me you can do nothing."

John 15:5 NKJV

- -

Be of good courage, and He shall strengthen your heart, all you who hope in the Lord.

Psalm 31:24 NKJV

- -

I can do all things through Christ who strengthens me.

Philippians 4:13 NKJV

- -

Casting all your care upon Him, for He cares for you.

1 Peter 5:7 NKJV

- -

How can a young man cleanse his way? By taking heed according to Your word....Your word I have hidden in my heart, that I might not sin against You.

Psalm 119:9,11 NKJV

Therefore submit to God. Resist the devil and he will flee from you.

James 4:7 NKJV

- -

No temptation has overtaken you except such as is common to man; but God is faithful, who will not allow you to be tempted beyond what you are able, but with the temptation will also make the way of escape, that you may be able to bear it.

1 Corinthians 10:13 NKJV

- -

The Lord is my shepherd; I shall not want.

Psalm 23:1 NKJV

Prayer

- -

For we do not know what we should pray for as we ought, but the Spirit Himself makes intercession for us with groanings which cannot be uttered.

Romans 8:26 NKJV

- -

"Ask, and it will be given to you; seek, and you will find; knock, and it will be opened to you."

Matthew 7:7 NKJV

- -

"Until now you have asked nothing in My name. Ask, and you will receive, that your joy may be full."

John 16:24 NKJV

- -

Praying always with all prayer and supplication in the Spirit, being watchful to this end with all perseverance and supplication for all the saints.

Ephesians 6:18 NKJV

- -

Pray without ceasing.

1 Thessalonians 5:17 NKJV

Suffering

- -

By faith Moses, when he became of age, refused to be called the son of Pharaoh's daughter, choosing rather to suffer affliction with the people of God than to enjoy the passing pleasures of sin.

Hebrews 11:24,25 NKJV

- -

For to this you were called, because Christ also suffered for us, leaving us an example, that you should follow His steps.

1 Peter 2:21 NKJV

- -

Cast your burden on the Lord, and He shall sustain you; He shall never permit the righteous to be moved.

Psalm 55:22 NKJV

- -

For I consider that the sufferings of this present time are not worthy to be compared with the glory which shall be revealed in us.

Romans 8:18 NKJV

APPENDIX

The Four Spiritual Laws [1]

Just as there are physical laws that govern the physical universe, so are there spiritual laws which govern your relationship with God.

LAW ONE: GOD **LOVES** YOU, AND OFFERS A WONDERFUL **PLAN** FOR YOUR LIFE.

(References contained in this booklet should be read in context from the Bible wherever possible.)

God's Love

"For God so loved the world, that He gave His only begotten Son, that whoever believes in Him should not perish, but have eternal life" (John 3:16).

God's Plan

(Christ speaking) "I came that they might have life, and might have it abundantly" (that it might be full and meaningful) (John 10:10).

Why is it that most people are not experiencing the abundant life? Because...

LAW TWO: MAN IS **SINFUL** AND **SEPARATED** FROM GOD. THEREFORE, HE CANNOT KNOW AND EXPERIENCE GOD'S LOVE AND PLAN FOR HIS LIFE.

Man Is Sinful

"For all have sinned and fall short of the glory of God" (Romans 3:23).

---

1. Written by Bill Bright. Copyright © Campus Crusade for Christ, Inc., 1965. Published by Here's Life Publishers and used by permission.

Man was created to have fellowship with God; but, because of his stubborn self-will, he chose to go his own independent way and fellowship with God was broken. This self-will, character- ized by an attitude of active rebellion or passive indifference, is evidence of what the Bible calls sin.

Man Is Separated

"For the wages of sin is death" (spiritual separation from God) (Romans 6:23).

This diagram illustrates that God is holy and man is sinful. A great gulf separates the two. The arrows illustrate that man is continually trying to reach God and the abundant life through his own efforts, such as a good life, philosophy, or religion.

The third law explains the only way to bridge this gulf...

LAW THREE: JESUS CHRIST IS GOD'S ONLY PROVISION FOR MAN'S SIN. THROUGH HIM YOU CAN KNOW AND EXPERIENCE GOD'S LOVE AND PLAN YOUR LIFE.

He Died in Our Place

"But God demonstrates His own love toward us, in that while we were yet sinners, Christ died for us" (Romans 5:8).

He Rose from the Dead

"Christ died for our sins...He was buried...He was raised on the third day, according to the Scriptures...He appeared to Pe- ter, then to the twelve. After that He appeared to more than five hundred..." (1 Corinthians 15:3-6).

174

He Is the Only Way to God

"Jesus said to him, 'I am the way, and the truth, and the life; no one comes to the Father, but through Me' " (John 14:6).

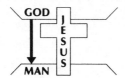

This diagram illustrates that God has bridged the gulf which separates us from Him by sending His Son, Jesus Christ, to die on the cross in our place to pay the penalty for our sins.

It is not enough just to know these three laws...

LAW FOUR: WE MUST INDIVIDUALLY RE-CEIVE JESUS CHRIST AS SAVIOR AND LORD; THEN WE CAN KNOW AND EXPERIENCE GOD'S LOVE AND PLAN FOR OUR LIVES.

We Must Receive Christ

"But as many as received Him, to them He gave the right to become children of God, even to those who believe in His name" (John 1:12).

We Receive Christ Through Faith

"For by grace you have been saved through faith; and that not of yourselves, it is the gift of God; not as a result of works, that no one should boast" (Ephesians 2:8, 9).

When We Receive Christ, We Experience a New Birth. (Read John 3:1-8.)

We Receive Christ by Personal Invitation

(Christ is speaking): "Behold, I stand at the door and knock; if any one hears My voice and opens the door, I will come in to him" (Revelation 3:20). Receiving Christ involves turning to God from self (repentance) and trusting Christ to come into our lives to forgive our sins and to make us the kind of people He wants us to be. Just to agree intellectually that Jesus Christ is the Son of God and that He died on the cross for our sins is not enough. Nor is it enough to have an emotional experience. We receive Jesus Christ by faith, as an act of the will.

These two circles represent two kinds of lives:

SELF-DIRECTED LIFE

S — Self is on the throne

✝ — Christ is outside the life

• — Interests are directed by self, often resulting in discord and frustration

CHRIST-DIRECTED LIFE

✝ — Christ is in the life and on the throne

S — Self is yielding to Christ

• — Interests are directed by Christ, resulting in harmony with God's plan

Which circle best represents your life? Which circle would you like to have represent your life? The following explains how you can receive Christ:

You Can Receive Christ Right Now By Faith Through Prayer

(Prayer is talking with God)

God knows your heart and is not so concerned with your words as He is with the attitude of your heart. The following is a suggested prayer:

"Lord Jesus, I need You. Thank You for dying on the cross for my sins. I open the door of my life and receive You as my Savior and Lord. Thank You for forgiving my sins and giving me eternal life. Take control of the throne of my life. Make me the kind of person You want me to be."

Does this prayer express the desire of your heart?

If it does, pray this prayer right now, and Christ will come into your life, as He promised.

How to Know That Christ Is in Your Life

Did you receive Christ into your life? According to His promise in Revelation 3:20, where is Christ right now in relation to you? Christ said that He would come into your life. Would He mislead you? On what authority do you know that God has answered your prayer? (The trustworthiness of God Himself and His Word.)

The Bible Promises Eternal Life to All Who Receive Christ

"And the witness is this, that God has given us eternal life, and this life is in His Son. He who has the Son has the life; he who does not have the Son of God does not have the life. These things I have written to you who believe in the name of the Son of God, in order that you may know that you have eternal life" (1 John 5:11-13).

Thank God often that Christ is in your life and that He will never leave you (Hebrews 13:5). You can know on the basis of His promise that Christ lives in you and that you have eternal life, from the very moment you invite Him in. He will not deceive you.